Selling with Synchronicity

The 7 Inner Shifts that Make Selling Fun & Easy

Ursula C. Mentjes

Potential Quest, Inc.
Riverside, CA

ISBN-10: 0988756706
ISBN-13: 978-0-9887567-0-0

Cover Design/Graphics: Dan Mulhern,
Dan Mulhern Design
Author: Ursula C. Mentjes
Interior Design: Teagarden Designs
Editors: First Edition - Amanda Johnson,
True To Intention

Copyright © 2013 by *Potential Quest, Inc.*
3410 La Sierra Avenue #F129
Riverside, CA 92503

To order this book, visit www.SalesCoachNow.com
Printed in the United States of America

Dedicated to all of my clients who have shown up through the power of Synchronicity.

It is so nice to know you.

I wrote this book for YOU.

WE have a lot of work to do.

In Memory of Roger Joseph Savoie...

You were loved by so many.

We miss you.

What Readers are Saying

"When people think of selling, they think of pain. But it doesn't have to be that way. In her first book, Selling with Intention, Ursula showed us how to simplify the sales process by being intentional in every action you take. In Selling with Synchronicity, Ursula takes it to the next level, showing us the 7 Inner Shifts we can make that allow selling to be easy and fun! From clarity to faith, Ursula will show you the step-by-step process to move from working really hard in sales to moving into flow and ease."

Craig Duswalt, Speaker, Author, Radio Host,
Creator of the *Rock Star System For Success,*
www.CraigDuswalt.com

"This is a great tool to access and understand 'selling' as natural and fun. Ursula has coupled authenticity and synchronicity into an honest and accessible way to share our Gifts and talents effectively and with integrity. Selling with Synchronicity weaves together insight, thought, and action, and teaches us how generate a clear pathway to personal and professional abundance."

Shajen Joy Aziz, Author of the Internationally
Acclaimed Book and Documentary *Discover The Gift,*
President of Transformational Inc.

"Ursula is like a sales angel. She comes to us through this book as our guide and protector, showing us how to grow our businesses through inspired action and without forced effort. Her goal is to make our business journey easier and to show us the role synchronicity plays in our lives every day – when you start to pay attention to it."

Martha Hanlon, Bestselling Author of
Customers Are the Answer to Everything,
Founder of Wide Awake Marketing, LLC

"Ursula Mentjes' Selling with Synchronicity breathes new life into the connection between the power of synchronicity and sales. Whether you're a novice, an experienced sales person, or anyone for that matter, you will discover an easy-to-use system that will help you generate sales, raving clients, and a sense of certainty that will elevate your life to a higher level. Ursula does this in a simple and clear way, and anyone can start applying her principles immediately."

Maurice DiMino, The Sicilian Mentor, Author of *The Art of Public Speaking: How to Kill from the Stage with Confidence, Character and Charisma*

"Selling with Synchronicity is the best book out there today! Ursula is a master at helping businesses make more money quickly and easily."

Jill Lublin, 3X Bestselling Author,
Author of *Guerilla Publicity,*
www.PublicityCrashCourse.com

"Ursula's clear and precise answers to the questions surrounding the mysteries of synchronicity resonate with my own experience. I was moved by how she so candidly opens herself up and shares her personal story in this book. Selling with Synchronicity will give you not only the understanding of how to turn your possibilities into realities, but also the action steps you must take. If you thought Selling with Intention was a game-changer, don't wait to get your hands on Selling with Synchronicity. It's a LIFE-changer!"

Bob Bare, Author of *More Power!* Founder of www.BestsellingExperts.com

"Selling with Synchronicity is the newest book by an author who has already proven herself to provide solid information on sales and transforming into a highly successful salesperson. I am a skeptic by nature and do not often take much stock, or pay much attention, to the intangible. In fact, I refuse to watch 'The Secret.' But when Ms. Mentjes speaks and writes, I listen and read. This book makes synchronicity and the art of 'selling with synchronicity' come to life in away that even a skeptic can believe."

Christina Loza, Managing Partner, Loza & Loza, LLP, Co-Author of *Internet Law: The Complete Guide*

"In Selling with Synchronicity, Ursula Mentjes has done it again — transformed the way so many people feel and think about selling and has dispelled the idea that selling has to be hard. By identifying the 7 Inner Shifts that people need to make, Ursula has created an amazing process to help people change their circumstances and get the outcomes they desire."

Gwen Thibeaux, M.A., Author of
*Embracing the Greatness Within:
A Journey of Purpose and Passion*

"If you are anything like me, just reading a how-to book is not enough to get you into action. I have realized that, for me, the mindset needs to be addressed, along with the how-to tips. In this compelling book, Ursula Mentjes does more than just address the mindset issues that keep you from accomplishing your sales goals, or any other goals, for that matter. She brings in the power of synchronicity and teaches you how to leverage it toward creating abundance, magnetizing the right clients, and reaching true success based on being in the flow instead of using force to get what you desire. Discover the magic of Ursula's 7 Inner Shifts that will help you transform your business and make selling effortless, fun, and easy."

Jackie VanCampen, Wise Heart Intuitive and
Founder of Wise Heart Within, Author of
*Letters to My Daughter: A Mother's Journey
of Healing and Transformation*

"Selling with Synchronicity is an empowering read. Ursula Mentjes skillfully identifies, addresses, and offers techniques to remove personal roadblocks – from expelling limiting beliefs and fears, to giving yourself permission to just 'be' until the next 'Divine Download' appears. I highly recommend this book to anyone who wants to be encouraged, motivated, and energized on all levels."

Peggy Ricks, Founder of First Impression

"Understanding how to succeed in sales just got easier! Selling with Synchronicity brings the flow of sales experience full circle. By combining the process learned from Selling with Intention and the understanding of universal flow from Selling with Synchronicity, the path towards achievement is undeniable."

Janise Graham, Owner of Entrepreneur's Insurance Services and Upcoming Author of *The Entrepreneur's Guide to Successful Business Succession Planning*

"Ursula Mentjes is able to bring the right combination of information, knowledge, and beliefs to empower us, as readers, to achieve our goals. Synchronicity as a principle has broad application and when applied to sales will lift your company to its next level without all the traditional work. If you want this process to flow and become easier, then Selling with Synchronicity is your secret weapon!"

Will Mattox, Business Acceleration Coach and Author of *The Future Formula*

"I met Ursula at a Business Event in the US where I was also speaking and spent the whole time writing notes as she spoke about the 'Art of making Selling Fun,' and then it hit me! Ursula had cracked the code to make selling easy for anybody with a simple 7-step process – a process which I'm glad to see included in her phenomenal new book!"

Sohail Khan, Speaker, Author, Joint Venture Expert, and Founder of The Joint Venture Group
www.Sohail-Khan.com

Acknowledgments

L ike *Selling with Intention* and *One Great Goal*, this book would not have been possible without the special people who have inspired and mentored me throughout my career and those who offered their amazing talents throughout the writing process.

First and foremost, I want to give gratitude to God for all that He has created me to be and for the signposts and messages HE continues to provide me to show me I am on the right path. I am clear that I am here to serve.

I want to thank my husband, Tim, for being my partner on this Synchronistic Journey. There have been highs and lows, and none of it would have mattered or held meaning without being able to travel this journey with you. I love you.

To Mom: For letting me ask all of those questions over the years and for encouraging me to be the seeker that I have become. Your belief that I could do anything paved the path that I am traveling down today. And thank you for saying it was okay to move to Colorado. I wouldn't have left if you hadn't said, "Go."

To Dad: You always wanted more for me — I know that. I am grateful for the opportunity to grow up on the farm. It formed me and taught me the value of a good day's work — and I was able to experience the beauty of farm life.

To Roger: Your smile, your laugh, and your joyful way of going about life inspired me to worry less and live more — in the moment. Thank you for always knowing what to say (or not say) when I needed it most. I miss you more every day.

To Kathy: Thank you for helping me to develop my love of reading and books. You had a profound influence in that area of my life.

To Mark, Shawn, Cassandra, Derek, Ron, Nikki, Talia, Logan, and Anna: Your unconditional love has meant the world to me.

To Loral Langemeier: For holding the space that more millionaires could be created, and believing that I could be one of them.

To Amanda Johnson, my Editor, Book Coach, and Soul Sister: Thank you for reminding me that there would be more than one book, and that I didn't have to try to pack it all into *Selling with Intention!* You have been an incredible source of inspiration, and you have always strengthened my belief in what I am doing. Thank you for living your purpose so that I and others can live ours. And on the days I want to give up most, thank you for asking me, "Okay, what else would you do?"

To my mentors, clients, colleagues, and dear friends of NAWBO, IEWBC, IWE, Inspire, the Live out Loud Community, and the BRC family: Thank you for all of your support over the years. Without you, I would not be where I am today, nor would this journey be half as much fun!

Table of Contents

Foreword

Ifirst met Ursula at an Author 101 event in Las Vegas. She walked right up to me, fearless, just before I was to take the stage and asked me to speak at her next live event. I thought, "Wow, this chick has got guts!" I immediately liked her. She demonstrated to me the fearlessness that entrepreneurs must have to grow their business.

I agreed to do her event without knowing a lot about her. This is something that I rarely do, but she impressed me with her resolve to have me speak. Again, that's not easy to do. Clearly, there's something you can learn from her about selling and getting what you want from this book.

My gut told me the event would be good — and it was! I was impressed with how things were set up and those that were in attendance. The audience obviously loved her. Right away, I saw an entrepreneur who was going to make it in this industry, when most don't. I also saw someone I wanted to mentor and coach to a seven-figure business. She has "what it takes," and I wanted to help her get there.

Having spent some time getting to know and work with her over the last two years, my admiration for her has grown. She has proven over and over again that she is not only good at what she does. Ursula is a woman of integrity, intention, and determination. She has a strong desire to help others make a lot of money, give back to organizations they care about, and live a very powerful, purpose-driven life.

I can't think of any one better to teach you how to make the 7 Inner Shifts you need to make to put more fun and ease in your sales process.

I personally know what happens when the power of intention and synchronicity meet a determination to help others solve problems. In fact, I cannot even count the number of times I have said YES without knowing HOW, and watched every person, system, and resource I needed almost magically show up. It's happened without fail. It just takes our action, our belief, our YES.

Yes, it still takes work. Yes, you will have moments where you want to throw in the towel. Yes, you have to be willing to do things that scare the hell out of you. But I can promise you, if you make these shifts, you will reap enormous rewards.

Selling with Synchronicity is not only going to help you sell more, it's going to make life a little — or a lot — easier for you.

My advice for you is to get this book. Read it. Do what Ursula tells you to do, because this book is about to change your life — and your business.

Sincerely,

Loral Langemeier
New York Times Bestselling Author
www.liveoutloud.com

The Synchronistic Spark

"Coincidence is God's way of remaining anonymous."

Albert Einstein

Holding my breath, I hit the refresh button yet again on the Amazon page. I felt like I had done this hundreds of times already today. Would this be the moment? Could this be the moment that my first book, Selling with Intention, would hit #1 on Amazon in the Sales and Marketing category?

Nothing happened. Nothing changed. Nothing moved.

"Be patient." The words echoed through my head.

But hadn't I been patient for the past six months? Hadn't I shifted the old self-talk every time it came up? Hadn't I let go of everything that could have stopped this from happening? Hadn't I stepped into the flow of synchronicity?

And then I saw the text from my husband, "#1!!"

I hit refresh again, and there it was.

Selling with Intention, my baby, my very first book, had just hit #1 on Amazon in several categories — including the Sales and Marketing category. Bestseller.

I let out a huge shriek and then a, "YES, YES, YES!" I jumped up from my chair to do a little dance. And then I sat down again, heavily exhaling.

"It worked…" I whispered to myself in disbelief.

With the help of clients, colleagues, dear friends, family, Tim, Amanda, and Janise, we had just sold a lot of books. In fact, we sold so many that Selling with Intention had just reached Amazon Bestseller status.

"How did I get here?" I mused, a small smile spreading softly across my face.

In 2005, more than five years earlier, I had written the first edition. Then I had schlepped hundreds of copies all around Southern California, speaking to sales teams and entrepreneurs — anyone who cared to listen. Anyone who wanted selling to be easier — and knew there might be a better way.

I had ridden the wave of synchronicity, and everything that I had been dreaming of was coming true right before my eyes. The best part of this story is that I wrote this chapter of Selling with Synchronicity six months before I hit number one. In other words, I chose this. I was "all in."

And now I want to share the power of Selling with Synchronicity with you.

Synchronistic Shifts

This book is not about me. It's about you. It's about making your journey easier than it was for me. My intention is to share my story, to show you how I got from there to here, and how I've learned to allow myself to ease into synchronicity to make the journey easier...for you. The truth is, the journey wasn't easy in the beginning. I have learned to make it easier by leaning into synchronicity rather than resisting the difficult things. Often those difficult "things" were simply roadblocks, or signposts, designed to send me in the right direction — to send me back into the *flow of synchronicity*.

In my first book, *Selling with Intention*, I shared ten principles designed to make selling easier while serving the client's best interest and highest good. The response that I have received from *Selling with Intention* has been overwhelming, and my readers tell me that I simplified selling and made it easy for them. I then wrote *One Great*

Goal because I realized that most people don't know what they really want, and I had designed a process that simplified goal-setting. Again, the response was that I had made goal-setting — and achievement — easy.

Business doesn't have to be hard. Selling doesn't have to be hard. We make it that way through our limiting belief system and lack of information. This is what I have been learning and teaching for the past few years.

My promise to God is that as I learn it, I will teach it to others who want the information, and so I decided to write *Selling with Synchronicity*. This book is about making selling — and business — even easier by understanding and implementing the 7 Inner Shifts that I will teach you. It is the step beyond *Selling with Intention* and *One Great Goal*.

There are thousands of books on the market that teach you how to sell and grow your business, but this book will help you align your belief system with your sales goals so that you can be "in the flow" of synchronicity and prosperity. Having grown multi-million dollar lines of revenue, and studied quantum physics and metaphysics for more than fifteen years, I know how to do it the "hard way," and I now know how to do it the "easy way." I want to show you how to do it the "easy way."

Let's be clear. I am not a quantum physicist. However, I am an avid reader, and I have read and applied the ideas of quantum physics with great results. As an NLP (Neuro-Linguistic Programming) coach, I understand how to release limiting beliefs and use visualization, and the power of my thoughts, to create my reality and help my clients create theirs. My belief is that I don't have to understand exactly how it works in order to harness the power of it. And you don't have to know how either. Please join me in that belief so you can get the results you want too!

Synchronicity is defined as "the coincidental occurrence of events" by Merriam-Webster. When coincidences begin to occur on a regular basis, we have to imagine that there might actually be something else going on.

I am and have always been a seeker. I didn't know that about myself for a long time, I just knew that I've had a million questions since I was born! My mom, Carol, still tells stories of how I used to pull a chair over to the sink while she was doing the dishes so I could stand on the chair, look her in the eye, and ask my questions. She laughs when she tells those stories today because she said she couldn't always answer my questions and wondered how in the heck I came up with them.

And I have been seeking the answers to the questions that I had about synchronicity. What is it? Why does it happen? Is it possible to make it happen more often in our business and in our life?

If you are intrigued by synchronicity like I was, and still am, and feel like it hasn't been working for you, then I want to encourage you to join me on this journey. Begin to ask the questions that will open the doors. By asking the questions, and sometimes living in the question for awhile, you will discover the answers.

Do you know what you really want?

Do you understand how powerful this Universe is and how much support is available?

What is your relationship like with money?

What do you believe about yourself?

Who surrounds you? Do they enhance who you are?

Have you built a community?

Do you have faith — and belief — that what you want is possible?

When you can answer these questions without hesitation, I promise that you will begin to experience a "synchronistic shift."

There is An Easier Way

Carl Jung, the granddaddy of synchronicity, defined it as a meaningful coincidence with the absence of causality. At one time, this was a little known idea. Today, if you use the word synchronicity, most people nod their heads as if they know what you are referring to. Since Jung wrote about synchronicity, numerous books have been written on the topic in an effort to explore and understand our powerful world.

Synchronicity suggests that there might be an easier way to exist on this planet — that the potential for ease, grace, and flow exists in every moment. Synchronicity whispers that we might be the creators of our own reality, our own meaningful coincidences. The possibility exists that it can impact our businesses — and therefore our sales as well. And, no doubt, it will also impact all areas of our lives.

After I wrote *Selling with Intention*, I kept wondering if selling could be even easier than that. There were times in my business and in my life when synchronicity seemed to happen more frequently than others, and I wanted to know why. As I paid attention, I noticed it usually happened when I was most in alignment with my mission and purpose, and I had made a decision to move forward with something. But I really wanted to know *why* and *how* synchronicity works.

As I read more about quantum physics, I became more aware of the possibility that while intention allows us to achieve our sales goals, it seems that synchronicity allows our ideal clients to flow to us. And so intention and synchronicity working together means increasing sales exponentially while doing less "hard work."

That sounds amazing, right?

But then the question emerges: Can we choose synchronicity when we need it the most, or does it just show up sometimes?

I found the answers to those questions. I have discovered through the 7 Inner Shifts, that it is possible to design a business — and a life — of synchronicity and flow.

Having watched this happen repeatedly in my life and business, and in the lives and businesses of my clients, I am sure of it now: Synchronicity happens when you are open to the possibility that things could be easier than they are now, when you are clear on what you really want, when you have decided to release the limiting beliefs about yourself, and when you have closed the "back door" on "what you will do if this doesn't work out." That level of clarity allows opportunities to just "show up" and chance meetings to turn into unbelievable opportunities. *Selling with Synchronicity* happens when we are in alignment with our purpose and what we are selling, when we are clear on our sales goals (or something better!), and when we deeply understand the problem we solve (or the pain we relieve) for our ideal clients — when we understand that we do them a disservice when we don't ask for the sale. *Selling with Synchronicity* happens when we take bold inspired action, lead ourselves and others, create and leverage a core community, shift our beliefs about money, and keep the faith.

Shifting into synchronicity is possible. I promise you that once you take this journey, you will never be the same. Instead, you will be allowing a magical and purpose-filled journey to unfold.

In the following pages, I am going to share the 7 Inner Shifts that I made in my life and business so I could reach my goals more easily. I am pulling back the curtains so you can see how it has worked for me. For me, life and business have become full of ease, grace, and flow, and as you will see in my clients' chapters, it's working for them too!

I am eager to share the journey with you, help you make these shifts, and make your sales easy and fun.

Grab your favorite journal and let's go!

You are about to experience a series of synchronistic shifts! Enjoy!

The Quantum Shift

*"The intellect has little to do on the road to discovery.
There comes a leap in consciousness, call it Intuition
or what you will, the solution comes to you,
and you don't know how or why."*

Albert Einstein

For a long time, I had a vision board that sat on a ledge in my office with a picture of the cover of the first edition of my book, Selling with Intention, on it. Under the picture was the word 'bestseller.'

Yes, I had a deep desire to have Selling with Intention become a bestseller because I knew that would mean that the book had impacted a lot of people. No, I didn't know if or how it could even happen.

However, by putting it on the vision board, there was a small part of me that held onto the belief that it was possible.

Over the months and years, I felt pretty hopeless because my little red copy of Selling with Intention was not moving very quickly toward becoming a bestseller. Or that's what it felt like.

And then a shift happened — and it happened at light speed.

The Synchronistic Journey Begins

When I was five years old, an angel appeared next to my bed at the top of my Sesame Street curtains. She looked like a doll-sized human with wings, perched there, sort of like the angel that goes on top of the Christmas tree. I remember thinking that I was dreaming, or hoping that I was dreaming, and I closed my eyes. When I opened them again, the angel was still there. I told my mom about it the next day, and I was so convincing that she actually became worried about me and thought I might be hallucinating or something. If I hadn't shared with her, I am sure I would have eventually believed that it never happened, that it was just a dream. But to this day, she still emphasizes how convinced I was, and I can still picture the angel so clearly.

At the time, my parents were going through a divorce, and I believe the angel was sent to let me know that I was not alone. We are never alone, and we are always being looked after. Since that day, angels have held a special place in my heart, and now I can feel their presence when something difficult is happening in my life, and especially when I am in the flow of synchronicity.

Most faiths embrace angels. They are found throughout the Christian Bible as well as other religious traditions. According to a 2011 Associated Press-GfK poll, 77 percent of adults believe that angels are real. I grew up in a wonderful Lutheran church in Minnesota, and I remember staring with wonder at the angels on the stained glass windows in church. I believed in angels, and my desire was that they would appear to me like they did to others in the Bible. But after seeing that one as a child, I never saw angels again, yet I have often felt their presence when I have needed them the most.

So, why am I talking about angels in a book about selling? I am beginning there because my journey into the magical world of quantum physics began there. In my experience, synchronicity gets a lot of help from the quantum realm that is all around us, all of the time. This is the realm where the unseen universal laws are always at play — like gravity. We can't see gravity, but we know it is operating, even when we are not conscious of it.

If you are reading this book, you probably already know about synchronicity and have experienced it at some level. You probably also know that it isn't by coincidence that you are reading this book.

As I have grown my sales coaching and training business, I have witnessed the power of synchronicity over and over again in my own business as well as in my clients'. What I've noticed is that when my clients have complete clarity and faith in their mission and goals, miracles begin to happen. Synchronistic events unfold easily and without a lot of effort. Many of my clients have moved from working extra hard to a place of ease, grace, and flow.

My mission is to help entrepreneurs and sales professionals like you understand the power of quantum physics and step into the flow of synchronicity that will allow your business to flourish and grow with less stress and no forced effort. Just inspired action. By doing that, you will be selling with synchronicity, and clients will just seem to show up out of thin air.

> **You** are an important part of my plan. Are you ready to take this journey with me?

What I know is that when entrepreneurs and sales professionals experience prosperity, they share it with others, and the world experiences a giant domino effect. I dream of a world that holds prosperity for all — whatever that means for them.

You are an important part of my plan. Are you ready to take this journey with me?

A Quiet Life

I grew up on a small family farm in Minnesota. We farmed sixty acres that my grandparents had passed down to my dad. Later, my dad purchased another twenty acres down by the lake, where he lives with my stepmother to this day.

Growing up on the farm was hard work, and still I enjoyed the daily commitments and chores. Well, most of the time! There's something special about a working farm. From the animals' expectations of care in the morning to the solitude of walking the farm at night, it was a pretty magical experience. I was also lucky enough to have ponies that I trained and rode. Some of my fondest memories from my childhood include riding my ponies through wheat fields after they'd just been cut and cornfields right after harvest. Fall was my favorite time of year.

I grew up in the eighties, and it wasn't the best time to be farming. During that time, many of the small family farms went by the wayside because they simply could no longer compete with the big corporate farmers. Today, the family farm seems to be experiencing a resurgence as we embrace the new era of organic farming and working more closely with the earth.

Because of their struggles, my parents, who hadn't gone to college, told my older brothers and me that we would get a good education and good jobs. There was a part of me that realized I probably wouldn't be farming, and my heart broke a little bit because I knew that I would miss this way of life. Yet I am so grateful that my parents engrained that in me at such a young age.

Knowing that I was expected to continue my education, I did well in elementary school and high school, enjoying most aspects of school. As I began to think about what I'd like to do with my future, I considered becoming a veterinarian so I could stay close to the farm. Unfortunately, I came to realize pretty quickly that being a veterinarian would require me to handle seeing blood, and that wasn't going to happen. I'm pretty squeamish! So I started investigating other jobs.

Since my parents had always told me I'd be a great lawyer, it was the first possibility I considered. I wasn't really sure why they thought I would be good at it, but maybe it's because I was good at arguing! It sounded like a noble profession, and I thought it would provide me with a stable future, so the thought started to grow.

Colorado Inspiration and Opportunity

After high school, I had the opportunity to attend St. Olaf College in Northfield, Minnesota. St. Olaf is a lovely liberal arts college, and I enjoyed my time there, learning and meeting life-long friends. Yet when I finished college, I felt really lost, not knowing what was the next best step to take, even after taking every career test possible in St. Olaf's career development center. My plan was still to go to law school. However, whenever I tried studying for the LSAT, I felt empty. A part of me knew that it wasn't the right path, but I didn't listen.

About that same time, I picked up a book called *The Celestine Prophecy* by James Redfield. The premise of the book is that an ancient manuscript is found that contains nine powerful insights about life. The book emphasizes making connections between events, using your intuition, and more, while following a fictional fast-paced story of what happens once this manuscript is discovered. Redfield's thoughts on synchronicity still echo in my mind, "Mysterious coincidences cause the reconsideration of the inherent mystery that surrounds our individual lives on this planet." After I read Redfield's book, I started to recognize the coincidences that showed up, and I no longer took them for granted. I started to watch for signposts along my journey, yet I still felt pretty lost.

One night, I was eating dinner with two of my girlfriends. We were enjoying our meals and a couple of drinks when out of the blue, we decided to write

> When I finished college, I felt really lost, not knowing what was the next best step to take.

down the top three places we would all want to move if
there were no obstacles.

We wrote in silence for a few minutes and then set our lists
in the middle of the table. We all laughed out loud when
we saw that Colorado was on all of our lists. California was
also on my list, but I didn't put too much thought into it.
Staring at Colorado on all of our lists, I felt my heart soar.
I didn't want to move away from my family, but there was
something inside me that said, "Go." I knew that I had to
move.

Was it just a coincidence that we all wrote Colorado on
our napkins that night? Or, was synchronicity at play —
outside forces helping us to get on our true paths?

A month later, my friend Jana and I packed our belongings
in a truck and drove to Boulder, Colorado. We were lucky
enough to be invited to live with Jana's aunt and uncle in
their beautiful home in the mountains of Boulder. They
told us we could live there for a month or longer for free.
Can you imagine? What a gift!

Jana and I had both been transferred from our jobs at Pier
One Imports in Burnsville, Minnesota, to our new jobs at
the Pier One in Boulder, Colorado. We were making $6.25
per hour, which felt like a lot to me after working in cafés
and doing odd jobs at small farms back in Minnesota.

Still focused on going to law school, I knew that if I was going to be able to afford it, I needed to get a job that paid more! Thinking back to the results of the career development tests I had taken — "you would be 'good' in sales and marketing" — I wondered if I might be able to get a job in outside sales that would then pay my way through law school. The light bulb went on, and I committed to get a job in outside sales.

In the moment I made the decision, something shifted inside of me, and I felt a strong energy surge through my tailbone. I didn't understand it at the time, but when I look back, I believe that the decision allowed my vibration to shift, and I had complete faith that a job in outside sales was going to show up. A deep knowing and a new confidence about what was going to unfold washed over me.

A few weeks later, I was helping a woman through the checkout line at Pier One, and we started chatting. She told me that she worked for an international computer training and consulting company and asked about me. I told her I had just moved to Colorado and was headed to Law School, as soon as I could figure out how to pay for it. When I mentioned that I was looking for a job in outside sales to help, she said, "You know, we are hiring new sales people in our Denver office. You should interview."

What? Did I hear her correctly? Yes, I had. I quickly grabbed a pen and a piece of paper, and wrote down all of the details. Within a few days, I interviewed and was hired immediately — the last sales person they hired during that time. Coincidence? I don't think so.

The first eight months were painful! I was terrible at selling, and I dreaded going to work every day. I hated filling out the tic sheets of all of the calls that I'd made. I felt depressed because I had taken this journey with the idea that it would help me pay for law school, but I wasn't passionate about selling or technology. Being honest with my feelings about the new job forced me to be really truthful with myself in regards to my plan, and I realized that law school probably wasn't my dream either. I felt lost and dreamless.

> Being honest with my feelings about the new job forced me to be really truthful with myself in regards to my plan.

At the time, I was selling into the government territory in Denver. Each day was a huge struggle, and I couldn't seem to get any traction. I dreamed of doing something else, yet I couldn't fathom what it would be.

There was a part of me that wanted to be an author "someday," but that seemed so far from my reality that I would immediately dismiss it. Where did that idea even come from? I mean, I loved reading books, but who was I to write my own?

Growing up on the farm gave me strong values and a level of persistence that most of my peers didn't have. Even though I dreaded picking up the phone and calling prospects, I did it anyway. I persevered. After all, throwing hay bales under a hot tin roof was hard work. Picking up the phone wasn't hard, just uncomfortable. I was starting to accept that this sales job was really all about living outside of my comfort zone, and there was a part of me that believed there must be a better way — an easier way — to sell.

Since I had no idea what else I would do, I decided to make the best of the situation. I knew that if I did well in sales, I could make a lot of money, and money would at least give me options, whether or not I went to law school. I recommitted to my sales goals and started working hard every day. Within a few months I had grown my sales to a steady $40,000.00 per month. I thought it was okay, but felt like I still had a long ways to go. Over time, though, selling was starting to get easier.

My confidence was growing along with my commission checks. As my confidence grew, I began to approach my clients in a new way. Although we were required to make 100 phone calls every day before we could leave, I began to see how making fewer calls of higher quality (more time on the phone) was actually more effective.

I had read every sales book that I could get my hands on. They all taught structured ways of selling that just didn't resonate with me. It seemed to me that someone had to lose (the client) so that I would win (and get the commission). That felt "off" to me. Inside I was screaming, *There must be a better way!*

At that time, Wayne Dyer's book, *The Power of Intention*, found its way into my life. Synchronicity was at work! I started to apply the idea of intention to the sales process, and things suddenly started to flow. My intention shifted from selling to serving and solving problems for my prospects. When I called them, they felt my positive intention. When I met with them, I knew they would become my client if I could solve their problem. Brian Tracy's book, *The Psychology of Selling*, gave me extra insight into how people think and how to help them overcome their pain and problems. Little did I know that my first book, *Selling with Intention*, was being born, although I wouldn't write it until quite a few years later.

Eight months into my new outside sales job, my manager asked to meet with me. He asked me how I thought I was doing. I said, "Okay," thinking that I was in trouble.

"You did much better than we thought you were going to do, so much so that we were wondering if you would be interested in taking on a new territory in Colorado Springs? We just opened a new office down there, and we need someone to run it."

After saying "no" a couple of times because I didn't want to move, I finally said "yes" because I believed it was my next step. In some ways, I felt like I had outgrown that office, and I wanted to take the next step. I wanted to have the opportunity to grow something "on my own," without anyone looking over my shoulder. My fierce independence and desire to "be the best" made me want to expand. My entrepreneurial spirit had been born.

Colorado Springs Intention

For an entire year, I drove from Denver to Colorado Springs every day because I was too stubborn to move. Through snow and fog, over black ice, and through the woods, I drove myself down to an empty office, got on the phone, and made calls. Cold calls. I remember a lot of long, lonely, dark days when I first arrived.

If you've ever made cold calls, then you will understand the depths of my pain for the first six months! Since I was my own boss in the office at that time, it was up to me to set my own calling goals and to achieve those goals on a daily basis. My managers didn't seem as interested in the number of calls I was making anymore. They knew I made the calls. Now they were more interested in my results and my profit and loss statements.

My results just kept getting better and better because I was selling with intention and using the power of intention. Before I picked up the phone I set my intention to get the appointment. Before the appointment, I set my intention that I would close the sale. And so I did. In one year, we grew that office to a million dollars in annual revenue. Not bad for a farm girl from Minnesota.

At the end of that year, my manager met with me in my office and asked me how I thought I was doing. As usual, I thought I was in trouble. Turns out, I wasn't. They wanted to offer me a promotion.

I set my
intention that
I would close
the sale.
And so I did.

"You did so much better than we thought you were going to do. We have an opportunity for you to take on a failing branch in Southern California. Want to go?"

My initial reaction was "No!" I didn't want to leave my friends in Colorado. Then I thought about it and saw what an incredible opportunity it really was. There was something about California that really pulled me. I flashed back to the time in Minnesota when my girlfriends and I all wrote Colorado on our napkins, and I had also written California. This really intrigued me. Without thinking about it too much more, I was on a flight with my boyfriend (now husband) Tim to California. Before I knew it, I was being introduced as the new branch manager.

California Shifts

There is something magical about California that makes me feel like I can breathe. Perhaps it is the peaceful mountains that I can see in nearly every direction or the expansiveness of the Pacific Ocean with a turn of my head to the West. Whatever it is, exhaling is easy. When I finally started to get settled in California, I wondered if I would ever leave.

So far, I haven't.

Taking over a failing branch in Santa Ana, California wasn't easy, but I took my intention with me. In fact, I set my intention to become the President of the company shortly after arriving. (I wrote about this more extensively in *One Great Goal*.) Over the course of three years, we grew that office from about $200,000 per month to over $3,000,000 with only five sales people. It was an amazing ride, and it was possible because we were practicing the principles of *Selling with Intention*, even though I didn't know that yet.

When I look back, we were also deep into the 7 Inner Shifts. I just didn't understand those yet either. We were clear on what we wanted. I was open to the idea that more powerful forces were at play. I knew how much money I wanted to show up (and it did!). I believed in myself. I surrounded myself with a strong team. I stepped up to be the leader of the company. And I kept the faith. Every day. And it worked.

When we hit $3,000,000 in one month, it was unheard of at that time. An average branch in a large market was selling about $300,000 per month. Why and how were we able to sell ten times that?

I believe it was through the power of intention *and* synchronicity.

Every time I set a new sales goal for the team, they rose to the occasion, and amazing events and synchronicities would unfold to allow that to happen. They met the right people. We created new classes. It just kept flowing.

Guard Your "Qwiffs"

My journey only got easier over the years because I read books with powerful information that showed me what was really possible. Catherine Ponder shared in *Secret of Unlimited Prosperity:* "Begin now to open your mind to the unlimited supply of the universe that is yours by Divine right…" When I first read her book, I read and reread that sentence many times. I wrote it down so I could look at it every day. I read it again and again until it stuck in my subconscious. As my income substantially increased, I started to *really* believe it. The truth is that unlimited prosperity is available for you, too!

Napoleon Hill, in his famous bestseller, *Think and Grow Rich*, shared the importance of focused thought, "First comes thought; then organization of that thought into ideas and plans; then transformation of those plans into reality. The beginning, as you will observe, is in your imagination." Reading this sentence was another "aha moment" for me. Again, I read it over and over until I started to get it at a deeper level. My thoughts were created in my imagination, and the more creative I was, the easier it was to create my reality. Desire and imagination led to inspired action. As long as I took inspired action based on what I wanted to create, things started to happen — quickly.

Then another powerful book showed up. *The Intention Experiment*, by Lynne McTaggart, captured the results of her work with visionary scientists who have studied the power of intention. As I read, I was literally jumping up and down screaming because everything she talked about confirmed what I had been teaching: When you choose the result ahead of time, it happens! McTaggart shared that whether it was through prayer, meditation, or simple thought, intention works.

We've heard a lot about the Law of Attraction over the past few years, especially because of the hit movie *The Secret*. In spite of its title, we discovered that people have known about the Law of Attraction for centuries, so I guess it wasn't really a big secret. However, for modern folks like us, it was kind of a secret. Well, at least it wasn't talked about in most of the business circles I was in, or even personal circles. I was taught that "hard work leads to results," not thoughts, and that if I worked hard, eventually

I would be successful; and yet that belief had been shattered over the years by the books I read and the powerful experiences I'd had.

One of my favorite new books, *The Science Behind the Secret: Decoding the Law of Attraction* by Dr. Travis S. Taylor, shows us how *The Secret* actually confirms what the world of quantum physics tells us. When a well-known scientist confirms that there is scientific proof that the Universe is really taking us on a wild ride, I pay attention.

Specifically, Dr. Taylor says that "qwiffs" are quantum particles pregnant with possibility, which change based on your observation. What?!? Yes, I know. Here's his explanation:

> "But no matter what the reality is at any given instant, when you have a new thought, you are setting up a new quantum state. With each thought, a new qwiff is generated that begins interacting throughout the universe. Your new thought continues to interact with the universe and with other qwiffs in the universe that are similar to it until a new entangled and common qwiff 'coheres' and becomes the next instant's reality. This is the essence and the heart of *The Secret*."

So what does that mean for you and me? It means that we need to guard our thoughts, carefully, which I've been teaching for years. I just didn't realize how scientific it was!

I always tell my clients to be careful what they are thinking about their prospects just in case they can "hear" your fears or doubts because, at some level, I believe they can. Dr. Taylor confirmed this inkling as well:

> "What you have to do is learn to train your thoughts so that you don't send out qwiffs through the universe that cohere with other qwiffs, that in turn generate the next reality that might be undesirable."

Guard your qwiffs.

Synchronicity Shuts the Door

On September 11, 2001, everything changed for our world, our country, and our company. Sales dropped overnight, and we started to struggle — as did just about every other computer training and consulting company. Companies no longer wanted to send their employees to training, they didn't want them to fly, or they just wanted to buckle down because of the changes in business. People were running on fear, sitting on their dollars, wondering what tragedy would happen next.

In 2003, the company was sold off. I was deeply saddened by how quickly it all ended. I started interviewing for other positions, but no one seemed to believe that I could run another company. Something about my youth and lack of twenty years of experience. The recruiters suggested that

I look into taking on running divisions in large corporations, but that didn't sound interesting to me.

My season with this company was over, and I was about to embark on a new season. There was a deep desire burning in my belly. I was in the "In-between" (more on that later), having finished with the company. I was in the often-painful place of wondering what was coming up next. Instead of fighting it, I leaned into the "In-between," I'm not saying it wasn't painful, but I leaned into it. Soon, the next season started, when one of the recruiters sarcastically said, "Why don't you just start your own company?"

> With as much intention as I could muster and synchronicity on my side, I launched that new company.

I could have taken that comment the wrong way, but I didn't. I was simply being redirected on my journey. Remember? Signposts.

So I did. With as much intention as I could muster and synchronicity on my side, I launched that new company.

Dare to Dream

by Amanda Johnson

"And now, you are all in for a treat." I took a deep breath as I reached for the little crystal butterfly on the table. I had given up trying to rehearse this part of the evening, surrendering to the fact that I was going to get emotional. *Yep, there it comes.* I felt the lump of emotion in my throat. *Words will never do her justice…*

"Six years ago, I met a woman who forever altered the course of my life. She needed help with her first book, and I needed her message of intention. I may have been a phenomenal editor, but I was desperate for transformation personally and professionally, and she was one of the angels Divine sent to remind me who I really am — a co-creator of my life with a Divine Intention to co-manifest. We had no idea that it was the beginning of a friendship, a business alliance, and a soul sisterhood. If it weren't for her…"

I invited her up to receive her surprise award — the first ever True to Intention Messenger Award — and I laughed when I saw her carrying a present up to the stage for me. The room stood to their feet in applause.

"Look at this, Ursula." I motioned to the room bursting at the seams with people. "This is possible because of *you* – because you believed in me when I didn't know how and because you are a master at facilitating quantum shifts."

I hugged her and walked off the stage to watch her do "her thing" with *my* audience. *My audience? Wow…who would have thought that this would be happening just two years later?*

More than two years earlier… October 2009

"Hey, Sis. Sorry I had to leave. Can you call me Monday? I need to talk to you about a dream." As I put the phone down, I wondered if she would be worried when she heard my voice shaking, especially since I had quickly bailed out of her first live event just an hour earlier.

I can't wait to tell her. I finally figured out what that phrase was all about. True to Intention is the name of a business that will use ALL of my gifts and the skills, tools, and strategies I have gathered along this crazy journey that she's been witnessing. I will coach people through the process of writing books — helping them to clarify their message and then hold true to their intention for the book while they are writing it. I just have no idea HOW to make that happen as a business.

Ursula was as excited as I thought she would be and invited me to join her mastermind.

"Amanda, it's your turn. Share who you are and what you do, and the challenge you would like support with today." I shared my idea, and she beamed.

"It's great. So where are you going to market it?"

What!? Market it? I don't want to market it.

"Ummm…I don't want to." I cringed at the thought of spending so much time at networking events. My family was struggling with a lot of challenges, and I just didn't feel good about taking time away. *There has to be another way…*

"Okay, then how are people going to know what you do?"

"Well…" I started and waited for the answer to come to me. I was surprised at how fast it came. "What if I established credibility with some of the people — business and branding coaches — who are telling people to write books to increase their credibility and profitability? They could just funnel people in my direction, right?"

When she beamed again, I saw a mixture of relief and excitement wash over her. *I bet she's seen this for awhile and is thrilled that I finally got it myself.*

"It's a great idea. Do you know anyone like that now?"

I paused again…waiting for the answer. "Oh my gosh!" I'm sure I looked like I had seen a ghost. "Yes! I do. And I already have credibility with her. I've done a lot of editing for her, and she has promoted me as an editor in her room before. But this would be a partnership… I'm not sure I have enough credibility to warrant a partnership with someone as successful as she is, but I could ask…"

Ursula knew I was thinking about the Secret Teacher I had attracted into my life three years earlier and worked with for the past three years. *How funny that I attracted her with the intention to partner, and now, it's here. I've done the work to heal my life, and I've gotten clear on my true purpose. I wonder what she'll say…*

"I bet she will." Ursula made sure I had no more questions and then moved on to the next person.

3 days after the mastermind…
March 2010

"Hello?"

"Ursula, she said 'YES!'" I just about screamed it into the phone.

"Of course she did."

"But I need your help." I asked her what she thought about the revenue split I was offered, and she said, "I think you can negotiate for more. She is putting a ton of people in front of you, but you are the one who has to sell them into the program and then work with them. You should be getting at least 50%."

I caught my breath. *Oh my gosh. What is she going to think of me? Am I really bringing that much value?*

As if she had heard my thoughts, she said, "Amanda, you are a genius at what you do. She does not have the same skills, and you would be adding tremendous value to her business. Ask for more. Here's how you do it..."

I listened, took copious notes, practiced, and then called to negotiate.

3 hours later...
April 2010

"Ursula, she said 'YES!'"

"Of course she did."

"And now I have another problem."

"What's that?"

"She wants to review my curriculum before launching me at the next event."

"Why is that a problem?"

"The event is in three weeks!"

Ursula let out a huge belly laugh and then asked, "Well, why not?"

"Ursula, I don't have curriculum, or a website, or business cards. I can't go into that room with nothing."

"You won't. You have three weeks. How can I support you?"

3 weeks later...
April 2010

Three weeks later, I had a logo, a website, business cards, and seventy pages of curriculum. I stood in front of a room full of 150 people, delivered my presentation, and sold people into our program. It was nothing short of a miracle — true evidence that this was my Divine Intention, and I didn't need to know the HOW, just the WHAT and the WHY.

I made more money that weekend than I had in the two years prior...combined. And I turned a portion of it around and invested in an opportunity to co-author a chapter with the Secret Teacher. I had no idea that two years later, I would be launching that book from *my* stage, with the Secret Teacher and four of *my* messengers.

I had no idea that I would streamline my coaching process with retreats and transformational coaching programs, that I would partner with Ursula and other business experts to teach my budding messengers how to build businesses and become transformational speakers and coaches, that I would create a book production program and team to walk the books through to completion and facilitate launch kits with websites and branded materials, and especially, that more than two hundred people would show up for the big launch event.

I had no idea that the quantum shifts would continue, or that they would force me to look inward and dig deeper, to trust Divine like I had never trusted before, to wonder if I had lost my mind, and to continue to reach out to the angel who was always there when I wanted to quit.

"Okay. So what else will you do?"

She knows there is nothing else. She saw my purpose long before I did…

Dare to Dream
March 2012

I looked around the room, bursting with more than two hundred people, and then glanced up to the angel on stage…

I wonder what quantum shift we will work on next…

 As a Transformational Speaker, Bestselling Author, and Message Coach, **Amanda Johnson** helps aspiring or struggling speakers, authors, coaches...and now parents... change their lives and their world with powerful messaging. After years of engaging, clarifying, and helping others develop powerful messages as a Student, a Teacher, and a Master Writing Coach, Amanda uncovered her own Message (The Butterfly Approach to Parenting, now captured in her book *Upside-Down Mommy*). The decision to share it with the world launched her on a journey of transformation that quickly made her disconnected and depressed life unrecognizable. Realizing how powerful a Message can be — not only for the audience, but for the Messenger — Amanda integrated everything she'd learned from some of the world's most outstanding educators, transformational coaches, and heart-centered business experts, and grew her business by 250% in just 18 months. Today, she supports others in developing, branding, and monetizing their Message...and staying True to their Intention!

To connect with Amanda, visit
www.truetotntention.com

Letting Go and Letting In

by Doris Muna

"Hi, my name is Doris Muna." My words sounded labored as I tried to catch my breath. The events of the morning had been so odd, I think I knew that something magical was about to happen.

"Doris, it's a pleasure to meet you. I am Lynn. What do you do, Doris? Are you new in the area?"

"Yes, my husband and I just moved, and I love this area. In fact, I chose it because I thought it would be the perfect spot for the healing center I have always dreamed of building." The words bolted out of my mouth without my permission.

Why did I tell her that? I'm not even sure that's going to happen!

"Doris!" Lynn caught her breath for a minute, and a wave of energy washed over me as I waited for her to finish. She looked like she did not believe what she had heard.

"Doris," she continued, "I have dreamed of building a healing center here for many years, but I haven't done it because it all feels too big. I have been praying that someone would come along who could see and hold the vision with me." The emcee for the luncheon interrupted us and asked for everyone's attention. Before we gave it fully to the stage, Lynn leaned over and whispered, "And to think, I almost didn't make it to this luncheon!"

"Me too!" I whispered back, wondering if I would ever tell her that I had not only barely made it to the luncheon at the last minute, but I had been ready to give up on my dream of the healing center for the last few months.

When I signed up for the Synchronize MasterMind in February of 2012, it was because I knew I would be moving in a few months and wanted that extra push to make sure that I didn't relocate to retire, but to continue my work as an energy healer...and maybe even work on finally building that healing center.

What's funny is that at the first mastermind in April, my dream for a center flew out of my mouth without my permission. I was going to answer Ursula's question about my sales goals with numbers of clients and hours worked per week, but I said, "I want to build the healing center I have always dreamed about."

Now why did I say that?

"Tell us about the center you envision, Doris," Ursula prompted while I looked around the room and found everyone's eyes glued to me, waiting for me to continue sharing my dream.

I took a deep breath and started, "I envision it situated in a large, permaculture, sustainable garden with plants native to its environment. The building itself has a half-dozen private healing rooms for healers and practitioners to use. In the middle, there is a large space to hold classes, facilitate meditation groups, and host speakers. The style is very simple, all built with recycled material and high ceilings. The colors are earthy with white accents. Accordion doors yield to the outside for large group attendance. There is artwork on the walls everywhere, interspersed with plaques naming the donors who helped to make the center manifest. The entrance to the center is warm and welcoming, with all of the upcoming classes posted on a bulletin board next to displays of Dorothea products. Of course, it has a little kitchenette and a few restrooms." My body was beginning to vibrate with the belief that this center was meant to happen. "There will be free weekly meditations, and then a myriad of workshops, yoga, dance, art, and healing classes. It will become a hub of alternative education and a place of healing for people and their pets. It will be called the Dorothea Center. In Greek, Dorothea means 'gift from God,' and that is what it will be."

"That's beautiful, Doris. And how can we help you make that happen?"

The coaching session helped me to remember what I already knew as an energy healer. It's important to write the dream down, map out a plan, and get into action to manifest such a dream.

But my oh my, did I resist working on the homework Ursula gave me! Projections and work in progress sheets.

Ugh. Maybe I will retire. I don't want to work hard anymore. I could be retired, spending time with my grandchildren, and...

With the move, I knew there was a good possibility that I would have less clients, have to start all over again, and miss my friends and contacts of many years. I knew the house we chose needed a lot of work and that I would not have an office to call my own. I had believed that I would cope, things would work out, and I would somehow be up and running my business within a few weeks of relocating. But that did not happen. I did not get depressed or upset, but I did start to let go of my dream.

By June, my dream was fading, and I was beginning to feel the impact in my business and my body. I fell and sprained my ankle, then my knee started hurting, and then my hip. All of my emotional blocks to moving forward were manifesting physically. And everyone around me, including my dog, Ms. Bella, was affected.

I knew I was going to let go of a lot of clients with this move, but this is worse than I expected. What was I thinking? Build a healing center at my age? Why did I say that out loud? Maybe I will retire. After all, I have done a lot in my life, been successful in all I endeavored, a healer with impressive results. So perhaps this is the time to fold and call it a day. Maybe the center was all in my imagination. Who needs it anyways?

One day while I was unpacking, I came across a stack of notes — two of which immediately caught my eye. One was a note from Amanda: "Doris, thank you for helping me heal and allow my dream to unfold. This donation is for your dream — your healing center." I caught my breath.

What am I going to tell her?

And then I picked up the next envelope that held a $2 donation from her young son Aaron, and I started to cry.

I know I can't let go of this dream.

I went inward and meditated, a lot. I asked the Divine, if he/she would handle all of this. I detached and took 'I, me, and myself' out of the equation. "I am releasing the 'how' with regards to this dream. Just let me know when You reach a decision."

There!

I let go, and went back to work with Ursula. I laid out my plans, dreams, and disappointments. I went deeper into the core issues keeping me from moving toward the center and began to uncover how to tackle them, and was grateful for the phenomenal support from Ursula and these like-minded entrepreneurs, who seemed to be more committed to my dream than I was at times.

I finally worked on that 'darn Work in Progress' homework, and I couldn't believe what happened as I began to intentionally write down all of my prospects and projections. It was as if the document began to vibrate the way my being did every time I dreamed about my center.

Amazing connections began to happen. I was invited to speak at one of Amanda's events and made a connection with someone who wanted to sell my products *and* hold classes at her location. That first one filled so quickly, I could hardly believe it.

And then I had met another angel named Carol, who graciously welcomed me to the area and introduced me to wonderful and kind people. When she had asked me to attend her luncheon, I had apologized, thinking there was no way for me to finish all of my errands in time. But then, my three-hour list was magically completed in just one hour.

This one takes the cake, I thought as I tuned back into the room at the luncheon and glanced over at my new friend Lynn.

I cannot wait to get home and email Ursula. She is going to be as giddy as I am about this synchronicity.

Lynn and I continue to talk and plan. We both know it will happen, as it is in alignment with both of our visions. She is helping me build the center of my dreams, and I will be the partner who will always be there, creating a space of caring and education to leave a legacy for the generations to come.

Please hold that vision with me, and come visit us at the Dorothea Center.

Doris Siksek Muna is an energy healing practitioner, consultant, and international instructor. She is also the author of *The Triangle of Health: Discover Your Healing Journey* and the founder of Dorothea Healing Essences. A member of the Touch for Health Kinesiology Association of America as a certified practitioner and instructor, Doris started using energy healing 20 years ago on friends and family and later started her practice. She uses a combination of the three systems of energy healing: *the meridian system*, *the chakra system*, and *flower essences* including remedies from nature. Doris is a medical intuitive, and uses all aspects of energy to analyze a situation, including Touch for Health, Flower Essences, Pranic healing, Paramitas, Herbs, Essential oils, and Feng Shui.

To connect with Doris, visit
www.dorotheahealing.com

The Clarity Shift

*"The future belongs to those who
believe in the beauty of their dreams."*

Eleanor Roosevelt

I was at a powerful conference for authors, listening to speaker after speaker share their bestselling books. When one of the speakers shared her story, I was riveted and knew I wanted bestseller status. Badly. I had finally become really clear that Selling with Intention's time had arrived. I knew I was going to make it a bestseller, and speak on that stage the next year, and inspire others.

And I had absolute clarity that my bestseller campaign wouldn't be like the others. They felt contrived and impersonal, and I wanted mine to be different...and easier! I knew there was a way. But what was it?

And then it hit me…

It was a new way — a simple way — full of intention and synchronicity.

The Business and My First Book

There was a time when I wasn't familiar with synchronicity, even though it was already at play in my life and in my business. I launched my first business, Potential Quest, Inc., a boutique business coaching firm, in 2004. Well, launch is probably not the correct word. I was getting my training in coaching at the NLP Institute of California while also finishing a master's degree, so it was more like a "fledging launch." My husband Tim was an independent realtor at that time, so we were both completely on our own, depending on our results to pay the bills. We had both come through a challenging time of moving from the corporate world to that of entrepreneurship, yet we believed that we were being led down our true paths.

Starting your own business can be ripe with challenges. Starting your own business when "you" are the product can be even more challenging. When you are the product, and your expectations are high, it can really take a toll on your self-esteem. This is especially true when people say no to your services because it is as if they are directly rejecting you. Let's just say that I experienced a lot of that in the beginning. Yet, because I was clear on what I wanted to create, more clients and bigger client results started to show up.

As I met (and coached) more and more entrepreneurs, I found that over and over again, they didn't know how to sell. They were afraid of selling. It made them feel uncomfortable, and they didn't want to appear greedy or "salesy." With my certification in NLP, I gained the tools I needed to help my clients with belief changes and fear release exercises so that they could reach their sales goals more easily. That's when my message became REALLY clear: Selling is easy when you can release the fears and limiting beliefs that are holding you back.

I found myself proclaiming my message over and over again, "Selling is easy! Selling is easy!" And then, one day, I realized that I couldn't say it anymore. I needed to write my book so that if anything ever happened to me and I could no longer say it, someone could still find the message. By writing *Selling with Intention*, I knew I could reach a wider audience. My desire was to serve others so that they would be able to experience a great life through entrepreneurship and professional sales.

> Selling is easy when you can release the fears and limiting beliefs that are holding you back.

Once I put pen to paper, the book started to write itself. When Tim was handling open houses on the weekend, I was writing. I kept writing for an entire year, and then I hired an editor from Harvard who had a nice website and sounded professional over the phone. At least that's where he said he went to school. He charged me $600.00, and I figured it was complete.

I asked Tim to look the book over for me, and he found grammatical and spelling errors everywhere. He pointed out that he wasn't a Harvard graduate, but he had found a lot of mistakes — mistakes that $600 should have found. I was beginning to think the editor from Harvard hadn't really done much editing at all. Note to self: Just because people say they have attended Harvard doesn't mean they really have, or even that they are any good at what they do!

I started to feel depressed, as if my book was never going to get published. While I had fantasies of it becoming a bestseller, the manuscript was collecting dust on my bookshelf. I knew that it wasn't complete. I needed someone else to help me. And then, in true synchronistic fashion, Alisa Griffis showed up. I met Alisa at one of the National Association of Women Business Owner meetings. Alisa is extremely intelligent, and I was afraid to have her look at my book because I thought she was going to tell me that it was worthless. She understood and explained that sharing one's writing is like sharing a new baby with the world for the first time. Every mommy wants to hear that her baby is cute, not ugly. I wanted to be reassured that my book was cute.

Alisa reviewed my book and sent me a list of things that needed to be changed. The baby wasn't ugly, but it sure needed a bath, and maybe a new outfit. Then she told me she was going to introduce me to someone else who was part of her team, and who she thought would serve me better. That's when I met Amanda Johnson, who is still my editor to this day. Amanda and I were on the same wavelength. We shared the same worldview. She was the perfect person to edit my book. She completed the edit on the first edition of *Selling with Intention* and did an incredible job, helping everything in the book make sense. I've heard that some people still have copies of the original red version of *Selling with Intention* (cover design by the talented Marcy Decato of Creative Solutions Marketing). My cousin contacted me on Facebook one day to let me know that someone was trying to sell a copy for $115.00 on Amazon. It was at a time when the book was sold out. I appreciated the confirmation from the Universe that I was on the right path.

To date, I have made hundreds of thousands of dollars on my book from the book sales and the various spin-off products. *Selling with Intention* has taken me around the United States and allowed me to speak on stage at some of the most incredible conferences in the world. I have had the pleasure of meeting my "gurus" like Brian Tracy, Loral

Langemeier, Dr. Ivan Misner, and others. The book has been my "Golden Business Card" and continues to open up doors that I used to only dream of.

Synchronistic Moments

I have a picture in my home that reads, "We do not remember days. We remember moments." Whenever I walk past it, I am reminded that we do remember significant moments like black and white still photographs in our minds. We don't really remember entire days.

Synchronicity is a lot like that. We remember synchronistic moments, and we don't always remember what led up to them, or how we got there.

A few years ago, I had the privilege of interviewing Dr. Ivan Misner, founder of Business Networking International (BNI) and The Referral Institute, for my membership community. At the end of the interview, Dr. Misner asked me, "How did we get here?"

At first, I wasn't sure what he was asking. My silence must have clued him in. He then repeated, "In other words, how did we meet? You know, the Butterfly Effect."

I didn't know. I explained to him that he had been referred to me by a colleague of ours.

"Okay," he said, "How did you meet her?"

I then traced back every person that I had met along the way — all the way back to the Yoga Den in Corona, California, eight years earlier. I had gone to the Yoga Den because I wanted to get in shape for my wedding and reduce the stress of my transition from the corporate world to entrepreneurship. Little did I know where yoga would lead and who I would meet. However, I did have clarity on the fact that I wanted to be a bestselling author. I wanted to speak on a national and international platform so I could reach more people. And through synchronistic moments, the path had revealed itself.

Knowing what we want — having clarity — allows synchronistic moments to show up. I like to think of synchronistic moments as those brief encounters when we connect with someone who will forever change the path that we are on. We don't usually know it at the time, and they probably don't know it either. However, they (or an incident) were put on our paths to point us in a new direction. Meaningful moments and signposts happen all along the road of life.

> Synchronistic moments happen when you are clear on what you really want. Otherwise, you wouldn't even acknowledge that the moment was meaningful.

In my humble opinion, synchronistic moments happen when you are clear on what you really want. Otherwise, you wouldn't even acknowledge that the moment was meaningful. We find meaning in moments because they point to something that we want to happen. Clarity allows opportunities to just "show up," and chance meetings to turn into unbelievable opportunities.

If you feel like synchronicity hasn't been working for you, then I would encourage you to go back to the drawing board and figure out what you really want. How many sales do you REALLY want? How many clients? How do you serve your clients? What is your purpose? Where do you want to travel? When you can answer these questions without hesitation, I promise that you will have a "synchronistic shift."

Expanding vs. Shrinking

I was recently speaking with one of my clients, and she was talking about her desire to allow money to come into her business. As she shared her story and what wasn't working, I could feel her energy constricting, as if she was getting smaller and smaller. At the same time, I saw money trying to get to her, but because she had shrunk so much, there was no room for the money.

So, I asked her to do something. "Notice your energy right now. Can you feel how constricted you feel? How small?"

"Yes," she whispered.

"I want you to imagine that you allow your energy to expand. Allow your energy to expand into the room you are in. Allow it to expand out into your neighborhood. Now, out past the stratosphere and now out into the universe as far as it will expand." I waited for a moment before asking, "Now, how do you feel?"

"Great!" she exclaimed.

When you expand your vision that much in regards to what you want, you are able to open up to the opportunities and money trying to reach you. In fact, the money doesn't have to try so hard to get to you because you've expanded what's possible. I know that might sound "out there," but whenever I do it, or I have a client do it, it seems to work.

I remember when I received the inspirational idea to start a membership community. I kept feeling a sense of urgency to do it, but I didn't know how. So I took action and started to do some research on the technology that would easily house my community. I made the public announcement, created an event, and one hundred people showed up the evening of the launch. Almost 50 percent of them signed up on the spot to be part of the community. When I got clear on my vision, the money just flowed in, and I was able to help more people.

Soul and Sole Purpose

One of the easiest ways to expand is to get clear on your Soul Purpose. What is your Soul Purpose? Why are you here?

Clarity regarding your Soul Purpose is critical to your overall success. We are all being called to do something important in this lifetime, and it is easy to feel lost about what that might be. But if you look closely, you'll see that you've been following a trail of breadcrumbs your entire life toward your Soul Purpose. It's not way outside of what you've been doing. Rather, it's the thread that ties them all together.

In *One Great Goal*, I spent a lot of time talking about finding one's Soul Purpose because I have found that when you find your Soul Purpose, and it becomes your SOLE Purpose — look out! Things will begin to happen!

Often people are trying to do too many things and go in too many directions. They don't trust their journey or what they are being called to do. And they don't get the results they want. When you know what your Soul Purpose is, and commit to it, synchronicity steps into play in a big way.

So what is your Soul and Sole Purpose? What is the journey you are on? Please know that there is no right or wrong answer. There is just what you are up to in the world. Another way to think about it is, "What would you do if money wasn't an issue?" The answer to that question often unleashes your passion.

Over time, your Soul Purpose will become your Sole Purpose, which ties to your Big Why, which we'll cover later!

Your One Great Goal

Recently, I had the opportunity to speak at a powerful conference, *Discover the Gift Within*. It was a wonderful event, and the program coordinator asked me to speak on *One Great Goal*. As I stood on the stage, I polled the audience, "How many of you believe that if you were clear on what you really wanted, you could achieve it?" Every hand went up. When I asked how many people actually knew what they wanted, there were significantly less hands. Instead, some giggles sprinkled around the room.

> Instead of moving toward our dreams, we settle. And then we wonder why we are unmotivated, depressed, sad, etc.

The truth is, most people don't actually know what they want. What does that tell us? It tells us that we probably have a general idea, and maybe we hear some of the internal whispers, but we allow limiting beliefs and fear to stop us from choosing what we really want. Instead of moving toward our dreams, we settle. And then we wonder why we are unmotivated, depressed, sad, etc.

Before he passed, Steve Jobs shared about the importance of clear, meaningful goals:

> "Your work is going to fill a large part of your life, and the only way to be truly satisfied is to do what you believe is great work. And the only way to do great work is to love what you do. If you haven't found it yet, keep looking, and don't settle. As with all matters of the heart…you'll know when you find it."

Believe me, it takes courage to choose what you want. There are many reasons, or excuses we can think of to stop ourselves from going in the direction of our goals. But these excuses are just the lies we tell ourselves.

We have all heard stories of people beating the odds to achieve their highest goals. My husband recently showed me a before and after photo of a man who got into amazing physical shape. In the after shot, he is in topnotch condition, with every muscle defined. Standing proudly, with a huge smile on his face, the caption under his picture read, "What's Your Excuse?" The man only has one leg. You get the point.

Bethenny Frankel, star of the hit Bravo series *Bethenny Ever After*, recently sold her liquor company to Jim Beam for a reported $120 Million — YES, $120 MILLION. In addition to launching successful businesses and being on three hit reality shows, she has written New York Times bestselling non-fiction books, cookbooks, and now a novel. Interestingly, she shared in a recent magazine article that someone had said "no" to every single idea she ever had. But she said "yes," and kept going. Now she's on track to be one of the most successful businesswomen in history.

We live in a time when anything is possible. Anything. And yet, people remain in their comfort zones, not taking the steps in front of them to achieve what they most desire.

Napoleon Hill, author of *Think and Grow Rich*, writes about people giving up when they are "three feet from gold." When faced with great obstacles it is easy, and even understandable, to want to give up. But what if *you* are just three feet from gold?

I certainly haven't achieved the level of success that I desire yet, and I don't obsess about it. However, I am certainly focused. If you ask my husband, he will tell you that I am probably one of the most focused people that he knows. He's watched me in action for years, with a front row seat in my career and the company I launched. Focused, I am, because I know what I want. I have clarity.

Knowing what you want, and focusing on one goal, gives you the rocket fuel you need to get off the ground. This doesn't mean you lose sight of other important things in your life, like relationships. Tim and I have a beautiful relationship. It is my top priority and will continue to be. I know that great relationships are a significant part of the life I am creating — and the life that most people want to create — along with their achievements. Remember to keep that in focus, too!

So, what do you want to create? If you haven't taken yourself through my One Great Goal clarification process recently, then I am going to encourage you to do it now. Figuring out what you really want — your One Great Goal — will help you harness the success that you desire, especially when it is in alignment with your Soul Purpose.

The One Great Goal Clarification Process:

1. Write a list of your top 10 goals.

2. Cross out 5, leaving your top 5.

3. Cross out 1 more, leaving 4. Cross out 1 more, leaving 3. Cross out 1 more, leaving 2. What do you notice about those two goals? If they are the same, then combine them. That is probably your One Great Goal.

4. If not, then choose between your final 2 to discover your One Great Goal.

5. Ask yourself, "*When I achieve my One Great Goal, is it likely that all of the goals on my list will be achieved?*"

6. Now, write down 2 steps you can take right now to move toward your One Great Goal (attach dates of completion to each one).

> If you would like to order a copy of *One Great Goal*, you can do so by simply going to **www.salescoachnow.com** or you can download it on your Kindle through **www.amazon.com**.

Now that you know what you want, I am going to share a few tips to get you on your way:

One Great Goal Success Tips:

1. Knowing your One Great Goal is the first step. But now you need to "get all in" and decide that you will make this goal happen...no matter what.

2. Notice any limiting beliefs or fears that you have about achieving this goal. Write them down. Notice whether or not they are "really true"— or is it possible you are just making them up?

What would happen if you gave yourself permission to just focus on your One Great Goal? You can probably already feel the tremendous power that exists in choosing just one goal, rather than all of them. It doesn't mean that the other goals won't actualize. In fact, I have witnessed that, more often than not, by focusing on one, the rest of your goals will also be achieved!

When we focus on our One Great Goal, stumbling blocks and hurdles often appear. Our ego is always working to keep us safe — and it does this through all of those doubts and fears that rear their ugly heads each time we reach outside our comfort zone. Remember that limiting beliefs and fears are just roadblocks. By acknowledging each fear or limiting belief, and taking action anyway, you will be on your way to achieving your One Great Goal.

Day by day, step by step, you will get there.

Eleanor Roosevelt once said, "You must do the thing you think you cannot do." Decide. Get all in. Take the step. You are on your way!

Setting Clear Goals

I cannot emphasize enough the importance of creating clear goals. In my experience, the individuals who easily achieve their goals do so because they have crystal clarity. They have their One Great Goal. Accomplished author Laura Day wrote a compelling book called *The Circle*, where she explains that writing your greatest goal inside of a circle (literally) brings about greater results. She talks about entering *The Circle*, not only literally, but also figuratively in regards to how you are being, explaining that "the Circle is a sacred space where you commit to just one goal so you can allow it to easily actualize." Her concept is so simple and so clear, and I believe that is why it works for her readers. I used it just a year ago — and it was the same idea. It was like putting my One Great Goal in the circle gave it power. It just confirmed what I knew about having One Great Goal — that when you focus on it, you give it energy.

A clear goal should be written in the present tense, not the future. It should be believable. I always love to tell my clients that it should also be a stretch. I used to think putting timelines on goal achievement was important. Now, however, I think it is more important to put timelines on when you will take specific steps to achieve the goal — not on the actualization of the goal. What if the goal can show up faster than you have imagined it? What if the timeline keeps it from you?

In addition to setting clear goals, it is important to visualize your goal from the end result. In other words, imagine that your goal has already happened. You don't need to choose a date, just imagine that you are standing in the moment that your goal arrived. Don't see yourself; instead, actually imagine that you are in the moment.

Then, ask yourself:

What are the sounds that I hear around me?

What are the scents that I smell?

Whose faces do I see?

What else do I see?

Most importantly, what does it feel like in my stomach, my core area to achieve this goal?

Getting all of your senses involved in the visualization allows the goal to easily show up for you. I used this same technique (which is NLP based) to help my mom quit smoking after thirty-five years. She imagined herself six months in the future, in her garden with her dog and cats, enjoying the sunshine and really enjoying the pleasure of being smoke-free. Quitting smoking was one of the hardest journeys of her life. I will never forget the day she called me to tell me that her visualization had come true! She had stood out in her garden, smoke-free, with her animals, enjoying the sunshine.

And eight years later, she's still smoke free.

Visualization works! Imagine what it could do for your business and sales.

When God "Nods"

When you get really clear on what you want, there will be moments on your journey when you will have a moment of complete "knowing," often when you need it most. In that moment, you will feel completely connected to Spirit, and you will know that you are on the right path. You will know that even though the journey hasn't been perfect and maybe the ride was a little bumpy, you are still on track.

In May of 2012, I had the privilege of attending Team Referral's annual Big Event. It was their 10 Year Anniversary, so it was extra special to be there. Les Brown was delivering the keynote. Just in case you don't know, Les Brown is one of the, if not THE, most motivational speakers of all time. I was eager to hear him speak and to meet him after the event.

Right before Les was going up on stage, the founder of Team Referral asked, "Do you know Les?" I told her that I didn't, and I would love to meet him. She pulled me over, and warmly introduced me to Les as "another" inspirational and motivational speaker. "Another" made it sound as if I was on the same level. I gulped. *I love her optimism!*

Let's stop there for a moment. That was a "God Nod." Many people have told me that I am a talented speaker, or tried to speak that truth into me. It was always hard for me to hear. And still is. I guess it's because when you speak, you aren't watching yourself, you are in the moment, and you are delivering whatever it is you need to share. Some people will go so far as to say it is channeling and that you are letting Spirit speak through you. When I say channeling, I'm not talking about medium-ship or anything like that. When I'm speaking, I experience "Divine Downloads." What I often feel on stage is that I just need to get out of the way and let Spirit speak through me. I've heard a lot of speakers say that they share similar experiences, and we recognize that we are the vessel for the information to come through, not always the creators. The evidence of that is when you get off-stage, you don't always remember what you just said. In fact, someone will inevitably come up to me and say, "I loved when you said (fill in the blank)," and I don't remember a thing about it.

Back to Les. So, the moment she introduced me to Les, he said my name (probably to remember it), and then was about to say something else when a woman stepped in between us, handed me her camera, and said, "Will you take my picture with Les?" I grabbed the camera, and Les graciously smiled at me and into the camera. I snapped the shot and handed the camera back to the woman. She said "Thank you" and left just as Les' team grabbed him to go on stage. The point is, we didn't say more than twenty words to each other.

Les got on stage and delivered a powerful opening. I was intrigued and at the edge of my seat when he paused and said that he was so glad to be there, especially since there were two aspiring speakers in the room, and whenever he can inspire aspiring speakers, he does. And then he named a man on the other side of the room, who stood up. And then he said, "And Ursula. Where is Ursula? Stand up!"

I stood up and waved. He smiled and said, "Yes, Ursula, there you are." He said a few words of encouragement and then continued with his keynote.

My inner spirit was jumping up and down with joy! It had been a difficult week for several reasons, and I had been questioning my path, my business, everything. It felt like things weren't happening very quickly — like everything had come to a screeching halt. I don't remember exactly what had happened, but I was feeling discouraged and had been praying for more clarity, so I would know the next step. So I could get a vision of what was to come. And somehow, I felt like I knew Les, and his acknowledgement of me as a speaker reminded me in that moment that I was on track.

> I have also learned to lean into those cycles to allow the next thing to emerge. God nods and shows me the next step.

Over the course of my time as an entrepreneur, I have come to realize that things happen in cycles, just like in nature. Now, I can feel things coming to an end in my business — cycles of relationships, organizations, clients, programs, etc. — and I have come to accept them as a normal part of my business. I have also learned to lean into those cycles to allow the next thing to emerge. God nods and shows me the next step.

The moment that Les acknowledged me from the stage as a speaker, my heart soared, and I suddenly saw a picture in my head of what was coming next. Ah, clarity! And a level of peace washed over me that I hadn't felt in a while. Les kept saying throughout his keynote that he was speaking to our subconscious, to our souls, and I could feel it as my vibration rose and my hope expanded.

I was grateful for the "God Nod." They happen to us all of the time, the question is, are you paying attention?

Clarity in Motion

by Yolanda Mason

Who knew this could happen in just two months?

I looked around the room at the grateful entrepreneurs. Their faces were warm with gratitude and the applause confirmed that I had finally found my path — a business with services that offered the perfect combination of every skill and insight I had received along my apparently disjointed journey.

She's been bugging me for two years, and now I finally see why. She just saw this before I did. It all started that day at her event…

"I believe in a world where people are living in their Soul Purpose, sharing their gifts with the world, enjoying prosperity because of it, and giving back to the causes and organizations that mean the most to them. When entrepreneurs and sales professionals make money, they do great things with it. Are you ready to make more money and do more great things?"

This lady is speaking my language. I've always wanted to make more money so I could help others.

I looked around at the room full of entrepreneurs applauding this beautiful and obviously brilliant young woman and suddenly felt grateful that I had been chosen to attend Sales Coach Now-LIVE on behalf of Estrada Strategies, the CEO Training Company I was working for at the time.

What do I love to do? What are my gifts?

I pulled out a piece of paper and started taking notes.

I really love what I'm doing, and I'm good at it. It is obviously one of my gifts to help business owners see what they do not see and develop processes to support their goals. I enjoy strategizing, coaching, and supporting, but I can't see myself doing it this way forever.

The rest of the event was amazing, and I knew I had to work with her to get clearer about what was ahead, so I signed up for Quantum Leap.

What am I being called to do? What is my assignment? What are my God-given gifts that I can share with the world and live prosperously through? I am going to work with this woman and figure it out!

The first Quantum Leap was amazing. Surrounded by other excited entrepreneurs, I felt at home and ready for whatever was coming.

"Yolanda, it's your turn. Who are you? And what problem do you solve for people?"

"Well, I am a CEO Coach at Estrada Strategies, and through my work there, I help business owners discover their next move, grow their companies, and create the systems and processes to support that growth, and…" I paused, wondering why I felt compelled to share this information: "I'm also a photographer."

The whole room seemed to cock their heads sideways at me, but Ursula smiled.

"So, is it a business? Do you get paid for photography, or is it a hobby?"

"No, I get paid. In fact, I've had a ton of opportunities coming my way in the last few weeks. Easy money, and it feeds my creativity."

"So, what do you think about going toward EASY and just doing the photography?"

Something happened in me when she said it. Part of me felt a *YES* and the other part of me said, "But I love what I do with the coaching. I know I'm supposed to be doing that too. I can't see how these two things fit together."

"It's something to think about, especially if the money is flowing easily there and not in the other place."

Ursula reinforced that photography may be an untapped gift holding much opportunity. Not immediately seeing how I could monetize the gift or change gears with where I was in the coaching, I agreed to consider it.

I think we're on to something.

Several months later, I had the opportunity to capture another event where Ursula was speaking. Amanda Johnson hosted her first Dare to Dream event, launching four of her messengers who had just finished their books and were ready to share their messages with the world.

As I listened to the messengers, and captured their gifts on stage, another level of clarity occurred.

I have a message to share. Someday, I will be on that stage.

Six months later, I sat in a retreat with Amanda, working out the core message of my book. My deep desire to help young women who are being abused re-emerged, and we birthed the outline for a book that would help them develop and execute an "exit strategy."

Yes! This is what I'm supposed to be doing!

Fast forward just one month, and I am sitting in a room with Ursula, Amanda, and Karie (who was also at the message retreat), but this time, I'm working on my business in Ursula's Synchronize MasterMind.

"Yolanda, it's your turn. Who are you? And what problem do you solve for people?"

"Well, I am a CEO Coach at Estrada Strategies, and through my work there, I help business owners discover their next move, grow their companies, and create the systems and processes to support that growth, and I'm also a photographer."

I looked around the room, waiting for the same cock-eyed look I had gotten the first time I said that.

Ursula smiled, obviously turning the dial down on her intensity. This was the first time we had some serious time to talk about where I was headed since the Quantum Leap Mastermind. Most of our other interactions had been brief at networking meetings, where she would ask me if I was moving toward the photography business, and I would reply, "Yeah, well. I'm doing the photography, but I'm still coaching. I'm still not sure how they can work together."

When she sees something in someone, she doesn't give up!

"Yolanda, there has to be a way to marry what you are doing in photography with your strategy and coaching expertise."

"Yeah, and now I have this book I want to write, which is all about helping young women develop and execute an exit strategy."

Ursula took a deep breath, and I knew it was because it was just another piece of the puzzle that didn't make any sense.

"I agree," Amanda piped in. "There is a way to marry these."

There were a lot of possibilities thrown onto the table, none of which felt right to me.

"When you take people's pictures, what do you encourage them to do with those pictures?" Ursula dug relentlessly, and everyone else held the space for clarity. I could feel their intention.

"Well, the pictures become part of their branding, so I help them figure out where to put the pictures and how to leverage them to become more visible and then create opportunities for their business. Are they going to go on Facebook, a speaker's sheet, the website, etc…"

When I looked up, everyone was smiling.

"What?"

"Yolanda, that's it! Your media company is the part of your business that attracts people because you are out there, shooting great pictures, connecting with people, and booking other gigs. So, if you set your focus there and begin offering services that allow you to use your gift of strategizing…"

Still not quite seeing it, I replied without all of the enthusiasm I could feel from the rest of the group, "Yeah, that's good stuff. I'm going to think about that."

It wasn't until I was in the car on my way home that it hit me — so hard that I yelled loud enough to make Amanda jump while she was driving, "Oh my goodness! Amanda! This is what people have been asking me for, and I didn't know it! I have three people interested right now, and I bet if I put my packages together, this would be so easy! Oh my goodness! This has been right in front of me!"

Amanda laughed with me and asked about the message, and suddenly, that piece was easy to integrate, "I am a Social Entrepreneur, and helping young women trapped in sex-trafficking will be my cause — my give back."

A month later, I was still working out the possibilities in my head when I walked into the labyrinth for a morning dialogue with God. "God, is this what you want? I know it's supposed to be Brand in Motion, but I just want to know I'm headed in the right direction."

"Yolanda, you need to help people get their brand clear and consistent." He flashed the faces of the people who were going to be part of my team, and told me to start calling and strategizing.

The launch date was November 30, 2012. I had less than two weeks to plan and create the lineup of speakers for the launch.

In no time, I had my packages together and had launched Brand in Motion. Everything came together — the branded design, the team, and the support I needed to launch.

It wasn't the easiest process. I faced a lot of challenges and questions about whether I could actually make good money doing something that was so easy for me to do, but

I just kept moving. And two months after that first Synchronize meeting, I launched Brand in Motion, sold several community memberships, and converted a few to bigger packages to put my team behind their brand.

I know there is even more clarity on the horizon — that I have just barely touched the tip of the iceberg — and I'm so excited to keep clarity in motion!

 **Yolanda Mason** is the founder of YMM Media and Brand in Motion, companies that help businesses "get their brand off the couch" by helping them communicate their brand visually, strategically, and powerfully. Yolanda takes her clients' visual branding (photos, videos, online presence) to an entirely new level, creates a strategy to launch it on and offline, and then implements it. The end result is a consistent brand that showcases the true essence of the business owner and their company. She also serves on the National Latina Women's Business Association and the Abundant Business Development Advisory Boards, and as the Assimilation Director of Youth Alive at Abundant Living Family Church. She was awarded the Estrada Strategies Coach of the Year award in 2010.

To connect with Yolanda,
visit **www.ymmmedia.com**

When Courage Needs Clarity

by Karie Armstrong

Could it be this easy? Less than a month has passed since gaining clarity about the Platform, and I already have two people signed up for the first phase? I can hardly believe it! But then again, this is what has been happening constantly since I met Ursula. I get clear on the next step, and it shows up.

As I packed up everything to go home, I recalled the many times Ursula had facilitated clarity for me and synchronicity had taken over.

Breakfast Meeting — November 2011

Acting on a lead from a business associate, I registered for a "Women in Business" breakfast when I saw the topic: "Taking a Quantum Leap." I had been out of Corporate

America for eight months, but busy with the immediate projects waiting for me. Suddenly faced with the reality of a sluggish client pipeline, I had no idea what I should do next, and no one to talk to. Everyone in my life believed I was going to be okay, and I believed it too. I just had no idea what "okay" would ultimately look like. I had the courage to move forward, just not the clarity. I had always been the leader: If I could *do it*, then someone else had a chance of *doing it* as well. If I couldn't *do it*, people around me didn't even try. Just a little pressure, right? Right! I put on a smile and façade of well-being but felt incredibly alone. Knowing I had to be at this breakfast, and yet look like I had it all together, I invited a long-time friend/past-employee/client to come with me.

I will learn as I help my client. Façade firmly in place!

The excitement bubbled across the room. As we moved into the crowd to find a cup of much-needed coffee and locate some open seating, something caught my eye — a woman surrounded by a large group of people. My background and experience has taught me to gravitate to the most sought after person in the room to see who they are. I've found they usually have a message or a gift — or they need mine.

Moving toward the group, I noticed her blouse. It was beautiful, almost ethereal, with golden sparkles and flowing sleeves. Having no idea who this person was, I touched her shoulder briefly and said, "I love your blouse, it's beautiful." She said, "Thanks," and I felt the warmth of her gratitude as she made eye contact with me.

Who is she? I'm going to find out.

Seventeen minutes later, she walked onto the stage and took the audience through a series of exercises that brought me immediate clarity. But it wasn't just clarity about my goals — it was the clarity she facilitated about my beliefs about myself. Without realizing it, I had allowed my self-image to shrink.

When asked if I was buying a table for the State of the City event a few weeks ago, I actually said, "Um, yes...well, maybe not. I'm so used to being the Great Dane in the room, I'm trying to figure out how to be a Chihuahua." No more small thinking. By this time next year, I will have: 1) opened a brick and mortar business, 2) facilitated a training series under my own brand, and 3) shared a stage with Ursula.

I went home excited, but within weeks, the clarity was gone. It's that space Ursula helped me recognize as the "In-between." Having spent almost three decades in shopping center management and retail, I found myself moving into the Christmas season for the very first time without the mania and intense schedule that arrived along with Santa at the photo booth.

How am I going to get through this? I should be enjoying this time with my family, yet I am miserable. And then the answer came through loud and clear one night as I drove home looking out at the vast Pacific Ocean. *"Forgive yourself, Karie. Stop punishing yourself for choosing a new path. No more condemning yourself to playing small. You are a Great Dane by nature, not because of the positions you've held or the companies you've worked for."*

I immediately called the Chamber and committed to purchasing a table for the big event. I enjoyed my holiday season while moving through the rest of my grief. And as the New Year rolled over, I took action on one of my goals and found the perfect brick and mortar office.

Six weeks later, I found myself at Ursula's Sales Coach Now-LIVE event, getting more clarity, not only about where I was going, but about who I was going with.

This is the community in which I want to play and grow. There were a few people who really stood out to me, one of whom was Amanda, and I put her on the list of "people to get to know and share a stage with."

It only took a few weeks for synchronicity to happen. The local Chamber of Commerce asked me to chair a conference. I said yes under a couple of conditions: first, I wanted to be one of the speakers, and second, I wanted to take the first crack at filling the speaking slots. I told the group that it was imperative that if my choices wanted to participate, we needed to do everything possible to accommodate their availability. My intention was for Ursula to keynote and Amanda to be one of the breakout speakers. I wanted their messages to be heard by as many people as possible. They both said yes.

But more clarity was on the way to help with that third goal. Synchronistically, clients kept showing up with needs that required me to reach into the talent pool of Ursula's community. Several wanted to write books, which required me to reach out to Amanda. What it didn't require, however, was for me to blab to Amanda that I also intended to write a book one day. But I did…and then back-pedaled, "It will be awhile."

"In the meantime, would you like to help at my next event?" she asked.

My soul knew that it needed something in her community. And I got it. I not only clarified and confirmed my direction once again, but I allowed myself to be seen and peeled off the happy façade to share my fears and insecurities in a safe place. I also got a loud message that I needed to attend Amanda's message clarification retreat to uncover my brand and make it memorable. Again, synchronicity was at play. Moved by my vulnerability in the room (much to my surprise!), Ursula contacted me after the event and asked me to bring my expertise to her community as well as join the Synchronize MasterMind.

Wow! This is really happening…

Only two months later, after sharing the stage with both Amanda and Ursula at the Chamber conference, and boldly revealing to the public for the first time that I had actually *lost* my job, I found myself at the first Synchronize meeting.

We went through Ursula's One Great Goal process again – the exercise that had jolted me into motion ten months prior. I filled out my sheet with goals and began crossing them off systematically. I circled one and drew an arrow with the word "later" to the right.

I'm not ready for that one.

I came up with my answer, and when it was my turn, I shared the safe, reasonable, attainable, small goal. But then it happened. In the crosshairs of Ursula's disarming gaze, I found myself acting as if I'd been shot with truth serum. "I also have another goal," I blurted.

Ugh! What am I doing?

"But it's too big. I'm not ready for it yet. Maybe next year." Blink, blink, gulp, heart pounding, I finally took a breath.

"What is it?" Ursula asked.

Oh boy, here we go with the brimming tears. That always signals that I am marching forward with my authentic-self, putting it all out there, no matter how terrified I am. *But what if they think the one thing that I really want to do is dumb? What if no one sees the value? What if they think I can't do it?*

I shared my vision with the group, realizing I had actually been working on it for a while but just didn't know it. In fact, the framework, for many elements, had already been developed over the span of my career. When I stopped talking, Ursula's sense of knowing radiated, "Karie, THAT is your One Great Goal! Why do you think it's not?"

"Because no one has given me permission…" I don't remember if I actually said that out loud or just screamed it in my head.

"When can you have the contracts written?" Permission granted.

"By the end of next week."

Ursula was silent. Blink, blink, gulp, breath. "Um… actually, I can get that done tomorrow."

Ursula smiled, the room exploded with support, and my dream was on its way into creation. I wrote the business model over the next three days and began putting the team around it. Less than one month later, the first client signed onto the first phase of "The Platform."

Clarity had taken my Courage to a whole new level... FAST!

After twenty-two years managing multi-million dollar enterprises in the shopping center industry, **Karie Najemnik Armstrong** rode the wave of courageous change and created her own firm, where she could combine her strategic-planning, team-developing, leadership, and coaching skills to assist businesses in growing, launching, or recovering from setbacks. As a business coach and strategist, Karie focuses on empowering the business owner to take the right risks, stack the right skills and actions, and get results. Her inherent desire to answer the question "Why?" combined with the determination and strategy of being a competitive springboard diver, more than two decades of bringing teams together to generate profits of more than $31 million each year, and award-winning success in launching new businesses at the SBDC uniquely qualify her to assist the business owners who cross her path.

To connect with Karie, visit
www.tkarmstrong.com

The Self-Belief Shift

*"Most of the shadows in this life are caused
by our standing in our own sunshine."*

Ralph Waldo Emerson

*As soon as I made the decision that Selling with Intention would
become a bestseller, the doubt showed up, pulling the light out of
the room, out of my imagination.*

*I picked up the phone and called my friend Amanda, "Am I
crazy? Can I really do this? Does my plan even make sense?" I
voiced my doubts, even though there was a part of me that knew
it was possible. She reassured me that it was all going to be fine.
It was all going to work.*

*And yet, the old beliefs and doubts crept in — Who am I to have
a bestselling book? Who am I to speak on that stage?*

And then I was reminded of Marianne Williamson. I heard her speak a few years back, and she shared her famous quote from Return to Love: Reflections on the Principles of A Course in Miracles:

> *"Our deepest fear is not that we are inadequate. Our deepest fear is that we are powerful beyond measure. It is our light, not our darkness, that most frightens us. We ask ourselves, Who am I to be brilliant, gorgeous, talented, fabulous? Actually, who are you not to be? You are a child of God. Your playing small does not serve the world. There is nothing enlightened about shrinking so that other people won't feel insecure around you. We are all meant to shine as children do. We were born to make manifest the glory of God that is within us. It's not just in some of us; it's in everyone. And as we let our own light shine, we unconsciously give other people permission to do the same. As we are liberated from our own fear, our presence automatically liberates others."*

Who am I not to have a bestselling book?

Who are you not to have a successful business?

Living Outside of The Belief Zone

Synchronicities were unfolding and phenomenal speaking opportunities kept showing up. I was invited to speak at Author 101 in Las Vegas, and that was a powerful moment because I had "claimed" my place on that stage a year prior while sitting in the audience. Suddenly, I was sharing the stage with powerful speakers like Loral Langemeier, Tom Antion, Brendon Burchard, and others. Talk about being out of my comfort zone — and my belief zone!

I was scared silly to get up on that stage. It brought up all of my negative self-talk and old fears about public speaking that I thought I had released. I called on one of my favorite coaches and healers to talk through it and let go of whatever was building up. She helped me tremendously, and I remember getting on stage to deliver "Extreme Networking" and seeing the audience — I mean *really seeing* the audience — their hopes and dreams shining brightly from their eyes. There was so much compassion in their eyes, and I could feel their deep desires to write books, grow their businesses, and make a huge difference in the world. The second I saw that, my fear left, and I remembered what I already knew: It wasn't about me, it was about them — about inspiring them to dream bigger, sell more, and move into prosperity. In that moment, my self-belief had shifted to make room for a bigger vision of myself — a vision as a stage speaker, not just someone who speaks to sell her products.

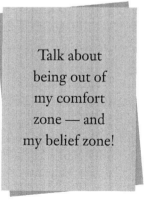

Talk about being out of my comfort zone — and my belief zone!

One person, in particular, I will never forget. I was standing on the stage leading the group through an exercise that I facilitate during "Extreme Networking." As each person was finding a partner, a man stepped in front of the stage, clearly wanting to engage. We'll call him John. John looked into my eyes, and said, "May I join you on stage?" I was momentarily surprised because most people don't jump on the stage during the networking, and I usually cannot participate so that I can maintain control of the exercise.

Something told me saying "yes" was the right thing to do in that moment. I smiled and said, "Yes, of course!"

He jumped onto the stage, paused for a second, and then looked at me, and said, "You are so powerful. You have no idea, do you?"

I didn't know what he was talking about. However, I felt the sincerity in his voice, and I knew he was trying to reflect something to me. He was trying to give me a message. He finished with, "You are different. Your approach — everything — is so authentic. Keep doing what you are doing."

I didn't know what to say, especially considering the level of fear I had coming into the event. I didn't want to disappoint anyone. I wanted to deliver something impactful for the attendees — something that would really help them. Later I was told that my presentation of

"Extreme Networking" and "Selling with Intention" had been huge hits. I sold a lot of classes that day, and I couldn't wait to connect with the people who had signed up.

What I hadn't expected was the gift from John, or the reflection and reminder from the Universe that I was exactly where I was supposed to be — even if I was terrified. I realized that it was okay to start believing in myself and the message that I had to share with the world. In fact, I really didn't have a choice anymore.

I am forever grateful for that moment because thanks to those who believed in me and my ability to deliver on stage, I grew two feet taller that day and was reminded of the signposts that the Universe gives us to say, "Yes, you are on the right path. Believe in the bigger vision of yourself. Keep going."

I Am Enough

Who are you? What do you believe about yourself? What do you believe about others? What do you want to believe?

Here is what I deeply desire for you to know: You are enough. You are more than enough. You are brilliant, and you were born that way. And, you wouldn't be reading this book if you weren't up to big things in this world. As Marianne Williamson shares, "your main job is to let your light shine."

That's it.

Easier said than done.

Showing up as your most authentic self involves making yourself vulnerable. When you put yourself out in that way, you are opening the door to ridicule, rejection, and all of the other things we don't like as humans. We have a deep desire to be included and accepted, and when we aren't, we get uncomfortable.

Living outside of our comfort zone is really about living outside of our "belief zone." It means that we are living outside of what we believe is possible. When we become uncomfortable, it can bring up all of our negative beliefs about ourselves.

Now when you get uncomfortable, I am going to challenge you to ease into it. Enjoy it. Why? *Because that is your opportunity to create a new belief about yourself.* If you are struggling with holding that new belief, then find someone to hold that new belief with you.

Launching my business made me question everything about myself. *Am I good enough? Am I really an entrepreneur? Can I really help them increase their sales?* After all, I had been a successful executive of someone else's company. Why couldn't I do that on my own? I remember attending my first NAWBO networking meeting. The speaker was a marketing expert with a successful (or what appeared to be successful) marketing company. All I could think was, *I have no idea how to market myself.* Sure, I could market and sell someone else's business, but I couldn't seem to sell and market my own.

A lot of people find that hard to believe because all they see is the end result. They see me speaking on stage and they think, "Wow, it is so easy for her."

No. It hasn't always been that way.

It is easy for me *now*. Well, let's qualify that. It is easy for me *on most days*. There are still opportunities and next levels that will pull me way out of my comfort zone — out of my belief zone. I know what that feeling is now, so it no longer scares me. It feels like I am standing on the edge of a cliff, without a parachute, and even though I don't want to jump because I am afraid, I know I don't have a choice. I cannot step backwards because my spirit will die and I will stop growing. And so I step off that cliff and then suddenly a bridge appears. It doesn't take me out of my game the way it once did.

> I remember going to networking groups and wondering why I was there as my palms were sweating, and I was having painful conversations with people who I assumed didn't want what I was selling.

It wasn't easy for me in the beginning. When I went from selling technical training to selling myself, I experienced a massive wake-up call. My fear levels went through the roof. I panicked. I remember going to networking groups and wondering why I was there as my palms were sweating, and I was having painful conversations with people who I assumed didn't want what I was selling.

Then I started to get a few clients and a few more, and I realized that the sales training and coaching I delivered was changing their businesses and, ultimately, changing their lives. Their sales went up. Their confidence grew.

And so did mine.

My old belief was that no one would want sales training from me because I didn't have twenty years of experience like the "great sales trainers" — Brian Tracy, Jeffrey Gitomer, Tom Hopkins, etc. But that was a lie. Every one of those great sales trainers got their start somewhere.

Even though my confidence as a coach and trainer went up, my confidence as a public speaker waned. Deep down, I didn't want to be a public speaker. I didn't like the feeling of being on stage, of everyone watching me. I wanted to hide in the back of the room where no one could see me, and I could be out of the spotlight.

A dear friend of mine is a powerful speaker, and he and I joke around regarding who used to "stink up the room the most" when we first started as speakers. What we mean is that in the beginning, we were ALL terrible speakers! Some people are more natural than others, but most of us learn by doing and listening to others. You become a great speaker through training, coaching, and experience. The more you have of all three, the more confident you become — and the better your speaking becomes.

By the way, the more confident you become, the more you will sell. In fact, when you are confident, your confidence will often out-shadow your prospect's doubt. Confidence always trumps doubt, and when prospects feel your confidence and believe you can solve their problem, they will probably buy from you. Yes, it is that easy.

Why am I sharing this with you? Because wherever you are right now is perfect. You are exactly where you need to be. If you aren't as confident as you'd like to be, don't worry! Find a mentor, coach, or friend who can challenge your limiting beliefs about yourself so you can stand in your strengths and be the leader that you are.

You are more than enough. Own it.

Done is Better Than Perfect

A lack of self-belief can certainly hinder your ability to close more sales. It can also impair your ability to get projects done, books written, and so much more. I've seen people labor over books, websites, and business ideas for years without ever finishing them. Why? Because they want it to be perfect.

When I wrote the first edition of *Selling with Intention*, it was far from perfect. I look back at it now and laugh because there were a lot of things that needed work in that book (not the fault of my editors, completely my responsibility!). However, I knew at some point it just needed to be done.

But here's the thing: That "imperfect book" made me hundreds of thousands of dollars. It opened countless doors for me. It put me on stages that I had only dreamed of. It changed my life, and it led to two more editions, a second book, and now a third one.

Where would I be if I had waited to write *Selling with Intention*? Where would my clients be if they had never read the book?

Done is always better than perfect! What are you working on right now that just needs to be "done?"

Finish it.

Silencing the Inner Critic

As you begin to work on getting "it" done, your inner critic might rear its ugly head. *Yes, but even if you finish the book, you won't be successful. Yes, but even if you become a speaker, you won't be very good.* And it goes on.

But the question to ask yourself is, "Whose voice is that, anyway?"

Your inner critic only has as much power as you give it. If you really want to change the conversation, then move the dial in your head. Remember, you are in charge of the station that you listen to in your head. You can "stop the show" that's playing and decide to tune into something else at any time.

> Your inner critic only has as much power as you give it.

What to tune into? Your cheerleader station, of course! I mean that. I used to tune into my inner critic before I went on stage. But now I consciously choose to tune into my personal cheerleader. It's my own voice questioning the critic and spinning me up into something better. In other words, when the inner critic starts to talk, it can take you down a dark rabbit hole, moving you from what is possible to the impossible world of "I'm not good enough."

When you notice that you are beginning to spiral downward, call on your cheerleader and reverse those thoughts. For example, when I hear in my head, *Oh no, you are going to stink up the stage today. You are so nervous you aren't going to make sense*, I change the station and get my cheerleader involved. She is happy to jump in and say, *Ursula, you've done this before. This isn't your first rodeo. Remember, this isn't about you. This is about the people in the audience that you are supposed to help. Get out of the way and KILL IT!* Note: "Kill it" is code for "Do your best!"

Once my cheerleader gets going, it's hard to shut her up. She just keeps spiraling upwards, which is great, because I still need her when I am on stage. *Ursula, keep going. You are connecting with them, they feel your heart, and they want your help. Keep going!*

You get the picture. Let your inner cheerleader help you spiral up and stay up. When you strengthen your internal dialogue, your external world starts to match it. As your confidence grows, you make bolder choices, and you ask for more for yourself because you know you deserve it. When you believe that you deserve it, you choose things that are worthy of you — including your clients.

Oscar Wilde said, "Be yourself, everyone else is already taken." That's the truth because in the history of the world, there has never been anyone like you, and there will never be anyone like you again. As your confidence grows, you will naturally give yourself more permission to just be who you are. You will become more attractive to others because we naturally want to be around people who like themselves — who are just being themselves.

The biggest surprise about speaking from the stage is that the more I allowed my most authentic self to shine through, the more people enjoyed my keynote or presentation. The more they enjoyed, the more I sold. I didn't become more authentic to sell more, but the less attached I was to the outcome and the more I just let Ursula shine through, the more successful I became.

On radio interviews, I've been asked what the secret to my success has been. My answer? "Being myself."

Be you. Believe in you. You are already the perfect you.

Rediscovering My Essence

by Nancy Ferrari

The room buzzed with excitement as the attendees for my first Essence of You mastermind group arrived, and my heart soared as I listened to them share who they are, what they do, and what they hoped to get from the mastermind. But nothing could have prepared me for one young woman's words: "Nancy, you always inspire me so much, and I know that whenever you create a program, I want to be a part of it."

Overwhelmed with gratitude, I held back my tears and responded, "Thank you. I am so humbled and grateful for your belief in me."

Yes, I am finally back in my creative flow, doing what I've been called to do, helping women discover their essence. Her words and her presence affirmed that I had shifted my self-belief successfully. I am amazed at how quickly it all shifted back into flow.

Four months prior, life had thrown me a curveball, which I have since realized was really an opportunity for me to believe in myself and my own essence again…

Pick yourself up, Nancy. I didn't want to look up. Everyone was gasping, concerned for my well-being. Staring at my coffee mug, I mused that it was standing straight up, still full of coffee, after such a serious stumble down the stairs.

Still in one piece. That's more than I can say for myself right now.

"Are you okay? Should we call 911?"

"I'm fine. I just need a minute." I stood up slowly, angry at myself for trying to carry my purse, briefcase, and coffee mug, and not seeing that my 4-inch heels were headed down a flight of stairs, not a ramp.

I slumped into my seat, embarrassed, and silently shooed people away.

I can't believe this happened, especially at an event focused on "mastering my million-dollar message." It was just getting good... I am finally clear on my message of helping others during times of transition, and am ready to master my delivery on stage. I've been silenced again, and this time, I did it to myself.

I was furious to find myself in the experience I had been reliving since I was born into the generation that held the belief that "children should be seen and not heard." The rebellious type, I always had something to say and wasn't afraid to express myself, especially in school. My teachers were not amused by my "show and tell" stories, and I was sent to the principal's office frequently. I was shushed repeatedly throughout my childhood and young adulthood, and it eventually took its toll on me. After decades of shushing, I just gave up. I lost my voice. I lost my belief in myself — in what I had to say.

It wasn't until recently that I had rediscovered my voice while hosting my radio show. It began as an experiment, but quickly turned into a career as others began to tune in and affirm my voice, my thoughts, and my essence. Thanks to the encouragement of those around me, including Ursula, I began to believe them...and believe in myself again.

Checking in with my body, I winced when I noticed the shooting pain in my back.

*Oh no! How am I going to continue on my path with this pain?
It nearly crippled me the last time it was this intense.*

I cringed, thinking about how this would affect everything.
I had been so excited to join Ursula's Synchronize
MasterMind. Ursula had believed in me from the moment
she met me, handing me a microphone to introduce myself
and share my newly branded business and the message of
Discover the Essence of You with a room full of people.
Caught by surprise, I stumbled over my words a bit, but
she asked the questions I needed to answer to get people
excited about my work.

Intuitively, I knew that Ursula would enhance my business
with her expertise in sales, and was attracted to the way she
brings out the best in me in such a gentle way. She is truly
my angel, and has always been there for me. That's why I
said yes to the Synchronize MasterMind, and shushed my
concerns about how I would finance it. Somehow, I was
able to trust in the process and know that the "how" would
show up.

A month later, we met for our first mastermind session,
and it was an amazing experience. We talked about accountability, our money mindsets, how to actualize our
desires, how we can support one another, and so much
more. I enjoyed the connections with the other women,
and it was a day of inspiration, and my call to action!

But two weeks later, I found myself literally flat on my face at this big event, feeling the aching increase in my body, and asking myself, *Why does this always happen to me? Perhaps the Universe is trying to tell me this isn't my path after all. But there were so many confirmations, and there was so much expansion last year. How could this not be my path? What's wrong with me?*

It took all of my willpower not to put my head in my hands and sob uncontrollably. The speakers at the event that day lifted my spirits, and I began to regain my composure as I focused on all of the positive messages, especially Ursula's.

I'll be okay.

However, as the day ended, the pain in my lower back intensified and, familiar with that pain, I knew that I would be sidelined yet again.

How can I continue to grow while in this type of pain?

After a few days of dealing with the pain, I struggled with the decision to continue the mastermind and called Ursula, "Given the circumstances, perhaps I shouldn't continue with Synchronize, as I need to focus on healing my back. I know how long this will take to heal, and I won't have the time to dedicate to building my business and implementing what you are teaching me while I'm waiting for it to heal."

"I understand, Nancy, but I believe in you and that you will heal. Take the time you need to take care of your back, and when you are ready, we will continue with coaching. You can also schedule your free healing sessions with Doris, as she will accelerate your progress."

Grateful for her understanding, I scheduled time with Doris. My confidence came back a little, as I realized that this fall was a message to slow down a little bit. Yet, I was still in an enormous amount of pain.

Suddenly, synchronicity kicked in, and I was given the name of a Bowen Therapy practitioner. It only took a few sessions to eliminate most of the pain, but he did explain that a repeated injury in the lower back area usually indicates a belief in a lack of support.

That makes sense. I never felt supported as a child. I know that the self-doubt and lack of belief in myself stems from this.

After my last Bowen session, and a powerful emotional release session, I scheduled another conversation with Ursula, as I was fretting over finances, realizing that my treatments were not covered by insurance.

"Although I am physically on the mend, I want to keep my financial commitment to you but am in a bind. I think I need to get a job to recover my losses."

"I understand how you feel, but Nancy, YOU are the job. All you have to do is what you were doing before your injury, and together, we will get you back on track. Abundance is waiting for you. Remember how much you have accomplished in less than a year. You are sitting on a gold mine. The world is waiting to hear your voice."

I am the job. The abundance is waiting for me. Somehow, something clicked. I knew she was right, and I said it out loud, "I am deserving and worthy to receive."

In just a few moments, I shifted all of my thoughts into empowering statements and recommitted to my mission in life, believing that I had what it takes to fulfill it. A student of my own teachings, I reconnected with my inner-self, evolved through the process by trusting that the right people were in my life to support and encourage me, and discovered my resiliency.

With renewed confidence, I opened up to synchronicity again, and the results amazed me. Almost as soon as I offered my mastermind group, it filled. I was asked to write articles for magazines. I shifted my radio show to a new network, and it wasn't long before "The Nancy Ferrari Show" was being heard around the world.

I know who I am, and I am living in my full power, embracing my gifts, and always living in gratitude for my blessings. I am experiencing the power of synchronicity and am grateful for Ursula Mentjes, who believed in me until I believed in myself.

Acknowledged as a leading voice of inspiration, **Nancy Ferrari** is dedicated to helping people connect, evolve, and discover their true authenticity and clarity of life purpose. In her signature coaching program, Essence: It's All About You, Nancy incorporates the principles of *Discover The Essence of You*™ and blends the power of personal development with the art of visioning, guided imagery, and intentional journaling to live a life of clarity. As host of "The Nancy Ferrari Show" on W4CY.com Radio and W4WN.com Radio on The Intertainment Network, she reaches out to audiences around the globe to focus on what's right in the world, featuring people who are making a difference. Nancy is a Certified Feminine Success Leader and Certified Vision Board Coach. Nancy lives in Orange County with her husband, Dominic.

To connect with Nancy, visit
www.nancyferrari.com

Mind, Body, and Self-belief Fit

by De'Anna Nunez

Sitting underneath the ornate chandelier at a table fit for a queen, I listened to the six incredibly authentic and powerful women share their updates and noticed how different I felt.

I feel like I fit in for the first time. I am worthy of playing at this table — in this community.

Incredibly self-assured and more focused than I had been in years, things felt very 'right' in my world. My usual scrambling-at-the-last minute behavior had not been seen for quite some time, and I felt as prepared as an Olympian at the start line.

Solid, holding my space with confidence, I handed off my projections and work in progress report with a sigh of relief and a smile. Without even a moment of hesitation, Ursula embraced my reports and kissed the plain old paper like it was the Holy Grail! Giddy from her reaction, I was even more delighted to be called upon.

What once felt like an overwhelming task and an impossible dream now feels and is…inside my realm of possibilities…only a few small steps from reality.

With poise, I delivered a report that explained the goals I had conquered since we last saw each other in person.

When I finished, the room cheered, and I realized just how far I had come since that first coaching call.

"De'Anna, what if it didn't have to be so hard, and instead of pushing, you could just allow?"

I don't remember how I responded, but I hung up from the coaching call and continued to hear Ursula's words play over and over.

What if I am making this hard? Why would I be doing that?

A scene from *Finding Nemo* (how many times have I watched this film with my kids?) flashed through my mind. It was the one where Crush the Sea Turtle was trying to convince Marlin the Fish to jump into the East Australian Current. Up until that moment, Marlin had no idea this current existed or what it could do for him, but after Crush told him about it, he had the choice — he could either keep swimming against the current by himself, or he could jump into the flow and get to his destination more quickly and with less effort. Hello? Was that really a choice?

That's what I feel like. It's like I'm watching Ursula in the flowing current of easy sales, and she's inviting me in, and I am just not getting it. Something is keeping me out here. What could it be?

The image in my mind reminded me of another area in my life where I had felt this way — like I couldn't get into the flow — yet found a way to overcome and step into ease.

Three and a half years ago, I made the decision to start running, and the first mile made me feel like I was going to die. Gasping for breath, I pressed on, determined to finish. I congratulated myself for the success and set my sights higher. I was 39 and told myself I would run a marathon for my 40th birthday. I increased my training miles and was getting ready to run my first half-marathon, but there was a logistical issue, and I had to run three miles just to get to the starting line. *Really?* I had trained to run 13.1 miles, yet it turned out to be 16.1.

But I did it, and the experience taught me that sometimes life requires me to make necessary shifts within my mindset to achieve a goal.

And then there was the first full marathon when, at the 22 mile marker, I felt the weight of self-doubt as if it were an anchor tied to my back. I had trained and fought to realize this goal, but the self-doubt of the past was weighing on me. *De'Anna, you can carry this weight with you, or you can leave it behind. Leave it behind. You are not that person anymore. You are a stronger, healthier person.* And then I had this amazing AHA, *I'm actually going to finish!* I finished the race, having overcome far more than 26 miles of running.

I conquered seven marathons with my new belief about myself, and then I fell…hard…on the Golden Gate Bridge in the middle of the big San Francisco Marathon. On my hands and knees, bruised and bleeding, I had the choice. *I can be embarrassed and quit, or I can finish. I'm not quitting. I'm getting up and finishing this race.*

The last marathon I ran, my pace felt less forced, almost rhythmic. I recognized my progress. I'd trained my body through thousands of miles, pushed myself mentally and emotionally, and shifted old mindset beliefs into new strengths. Minutes from crossing the finish line and attaining a personal Marathon record, I held my pace until the brightly colored finish banner stretched across the course. Surging forward into a full-out sprint, I passed one, two, three men and flew across the line with hands in the air yelling, "Wooohooo!"

That was almost too easy. What's next?

It was time for me to bring all of that self-confidence and the powerful self-belief I had gathered from running to my business.

Eye makeup running down my cheeks, I was in serious need of a tissue. People passing by must have been thinking I was having a meltdown, but really my tears were the result of an assurance that I am on the right path.

I know I need to commit to some serious leaps to grow my business the way I am committed to improving my time with every marathon. There is much I must learn, and the only way to expand is to continue expanding my self-belief. I am just as worthy of a healthy, thriving business as I am of a healthy, thriving body. This is just the next level, De'Anna. Press on.

As the sheet that officially signed me up to be a Synchronicity sister passed from my hands to Ursula's eight months ago, I committed myself to a quantum leap. I had been asking God, the Universe, and the vibration of gratitude to show me the steps I needed to take. Out on a limb, above a gaping thousand-foot canyon, I heard that inner voice that I have learned to listen to while I'm running — the one that whispers, "*You got this. You're on the right path.*"

When she took my sign-up form, she confirmed it was the right move by speaking straight to the chatter that had only been in my head, "De'Anna, it's a big leap, but trust me, it's going to be great."

And that, it has been...

Because of the coaching I have received from Ursula, I have learned that the process of growing profits and finding clients is simple — that by being faithful to the truth in my message and living through my own positive self-belief, I attract the right clients and can easily hit my sales goals.

Synchronicity has also rewarded me with the courage to make quantum leaps in a new direction. In just eight months, I have relocated my home and business from a place I loved, back to where it all began. Without even realizing it for the first few months, I moved less than a mile from my high school, where I was once a very different girl, feeling like I had to prove my worth to everyone. Necessary self-healing has taken place during my morning 5am training runs that could not have happened as powerfully where I was living before. Coincidence? I don't think so.

Because of the move, my children are surrounded by nurturing family members, and my business is in a geographic location that is optimal for expansion. Supported with the financial means to continue sharing the message that I am so passionate about sharing, my business has expanded into incredible new products and services that are allowing my clients to get the lasting weight loss results they have always wanted. I am reaching out regularly to broader audiences and using my voice to share the inspiration of good health.

Women are gathering around my dream and my one great goal of having a thriving Mind Body Fit Club chapter in every region of every state throughout the U.S. is already actualizing.

The process of synchronicity is so intentional...I get goosebumps imagining what lies ahead for me...as I continue to keep my mind, body, and self-belief healthy and thriving.

De'Anna Nunez is a happily married, glad-to-be mom of three, accomplished speaker, professional Hypnotherapist, Certified Fitness Nutrition Specialist, Certified Personal Trainer, RRCA Certified Running Coach, NLP Practitioner, and spirited fitness enthusiast. Her diverse background in Hypnotherapy, Neuro Linguistic Humanistic Psychology, Weight-Loss Therapy, public speaking, improvisational comedy, and professional comedy stage hypnosis qualifies her as a woman who not only does it all, but delivers it with her unique flair for life. Her clients include EMC, Mercury Insurance, Aramark, AFLAC, Bernick's Distributing, and The United States Marine Corps. De'Anna has successfully completed 24 Full (26.2) and Half Marathons (13.1) in the last three years — cheering, singing, and smiling all the way down the road. She is known for her 'Peter Pan' high kicks on the event course!

To connect with De'Anna, visit
www.burnyourfatpants.com

The Bold
Inspired Action Shift

*"Bold action in the face of uncertainty
is not only terrifying, but necessary
in the pursuit of great work."*

Jonathan Fields

Standing in front of the room, staring out at the excited faces, I felt the big lump in my throat. I was about to announce to a hundred women at a local community event that Selling with Intention would become a bestselling book in six months.

Note: I intended to announce it as if I was expecting it would happen.

Right before I went up to speak, I asked Amanda one last time, "I should announce the bestseller campaign here, right?"

"Of course you should!"

As I was looking out at the faces in the audience, I wasn't so sure. Taking a deep breath, I made the decision and announced it in spite of my doubt and fear, "On October 11, 2011, Selling with Intention will become a bestseller."

My words were met with loud applause, big smiles, and great expectations.

Not only had I made the decision and gotten all in, I had also announced it publicly to one hundred of my clients, friends, and business associates.

There was no turning back…

Getting All In & Make a Declaration

This is the shift where the magic really starts. You can know there are quantum possibilities and opportunities for you to increase your sales and change your life. You can get clear on what you want and the best way to achieve it. You can work on your self-belief and activate your cheer-leader. Yes, you can do all of this and still not get results without making *this* shift. And this is where I see the most sales professionals and entrepreneurs get stuck. They get all excited about the possibilities, clear about what they want, and begin to believe in themselves, and then they get stagnant and wonder why nothing is happening.

This is the shift where you start moving, and I'm not talking about baby steps. Baby steps are what you did to get to this moment, and those were great. But this shift happens when you "get all in." It's what happens when you see where you want to go, and you choose to close the door on every other possibility and move forward.

This is when you begin to take bold inspired action!

Your ego will want you to stay home on the couch and watch reality television, but it's time to make your declaration and MOVE! And I mean MOVE!

I guarantee you that this will be one of those moments when every fiber in your body will tell you to stop — that it's not possible, that it's too hard. And it's the exact time when you will need to push forward in spite of all of your fears.

> There is a time when we have to burn the bridge and take the leap into bold inspired action.

The Burning Bridge

I see it over and over again, and I recognize it because I've experienced it. When we set a powerful intention to shift our sales or our life, things begin to happen. Yet, there comes a time when in order to make it happen, we have to stop allowing there to be other options — alternative jobs/careers, failure, etc. There is a time when we have to burn the bridge and take the leap into bold inspired action.

And there are times when this seems to happen for us — when the world around us might appear to be falling away, when things might seem to be falling apart. Yet those are our opportunities to get committed — to use our One Great Goal to guide us to the next step that is *in* alignment with it.

Right before I moved from the Inland Empire to Orange County, it seemed like a lot of things were falling apart. As I've shared, Tim and I had lost a lot of money in real estate and due to those big hits, we were wondering how we could keep going financially. We had to make many tough decisions about how we spent money. I remember cutting back on everything and just being glad that we could eat.

Yet, I wasn't the only person going through tough times in the Inland Empire. We had all been hit hard by the economy, and the real estate industry was in shambles. Everyone we knew was upside down on their home or rental properties. A lot of people had either lost a job, a house, or a ton of money in real estate. Even though we weren't alone, it was hard not to feel alone in the midst of the great recession.

Strangely, as many things fell away in my life, I felt myself getting more and more committed to my purpose and journey. I got all in. Tim got all in. Soon, he was promoted, and my business was becoming more successful.

Tim and I came to the conclusion that losing so much had given us back our lives and reminded us of what was most important: *God, family, and health.* That was it.

Once I was all in, I let go of how I thought things "were supposed to be." I burned the bridge. I made public declarations regarding what I was going to create in my business and in my life. I planned my big event Sales Coach Now-LIVE in spite of the lack of funds in my bank account and started telling people about it. I created new training and programs for my clients without knowing where those clients would come from. I started working on my third book, even though I could have stayed at home panicking about what wasn't showing up in the physical world. And I told anyone who would listen what I was up to.

The world is full of stories of people hitting their "proverbial bottom" right before their dreams were actualized.

I was on a panel interview recently, sitting next to a well-known transformational leader who was the author of a bestselling book that had been made into a movie. She was sharing her story and the challenges she and her family faced getting the book published and the movie made —

putting every penny they had into it. She shared that they had almost lost everything. And then, right when they thought they could no longer take it, a major investor showed up, and now they are in the midst of more abundance than she could ever have imagined.

When everything appears to be falling apart, let go! Things aren't falling apart — the *way* is just being cleared for you. Don't be afraid. Don't put on the brakes. Keep going by taking bold inspired action!

Reconnect with Your Mission and Big Why

To get "all in," you must get really clear on why you are doing this (what problem you are really solving) and how you are doing it differently (what makes you unique). A lot of people struggle with leadership because they are afraid to be visible and haven't fully committed to their Big Why. They are afraid that if they really stand up for what they believe in, they will be ridiculed or ostracized. I understand that fear because I was afraid to stand up in the beginning as well — to really stand for something.

> "I dream of a world where everyone has more than enough money, lives a great life, and gives back to their favorite charities."

But as my Big Why became crystal clear, the fear left. I'm

sure I'm not the first sales trainer who wants everyone to make a lot of money, but I *am* probably the first who has stood up and said, "I dream of a world where everyone has more than enough money, lives a great life, and gives back to their favorite charities."

Yes, there are people who probably think my ideas are a little out there. I can hear them now, "Wow, she really believes that the entire world can have prosperity? Good luck with that!" But if I don't hold that space that is uniquely mine, who will?

And it is the same for you. When you are standing in what is uniquely yours, you will know it. How? Because people will start to quote you. I hear people saying, "My One Great Goal is…" and "I was Selling with Intention today!" Those combinations of words are uniquely mine. No one else is saying it quite like that, which is why I have pounded my stake into the ground on those words. That is my homestead. That is the reason I had to make *Selling with Intention* a bestseller and get the message to a broader audience.

Zig Ziglar's Big Why was about helping others. He said, "You can have everything you want, if you will just help enough other people get what they want."

So what is uniquely yours — what is your Big Why? If you

were going to take a stand in the world, a BIG stand, what would it be? What do you believe so strongly in that it would make you do things you wouldn't normally do?

As I have mentioned many times from the stage, I do not like public speaking. I never did. However, my desire to get my Big Why out to the world trumped my desire to play small and stay off the stage.

When you hammer your stake into the ground and really stand up for something, synchronicity kicks in. As you begin to communicate your message to the world and share it with others, your Big Why will become clearer and clearer. And, if you don't step up, someone else will.

I remember having this conversation with a colleague of mine. He was sharing how irritated he was with people in the industry who had been in business about the same amount of time that he had been but appeared to be much more successful. I asked him a series of questions, and it became clear that he just hadn't gotten committed to his Big Why. The others who appeared to be more successful were crystal clear on theirs and it easily drove their success. I watched his light bulb go on. It was that easy.

What is your Big Why? Why are you selling the products and services that you are? What do you hope to accomplish for others and for yourself?

Help Your Clients Take Bold Inspired Action

Once you are crystal clear on your Big Why, it's time to review your sales goals and make sure they are in complete alignment with your values. Remember, you are the leader of your sales goals. No one else. No one will tell you to get up in the morning and sell more. No one will tell you to get on the phones or hire someone to help you make appointments. No one will design your next marketing campaign for you. No one will make you do the thing you think you cannot do to increase your impact on your clients' bottom lines and yours.

It's really all up to you to boldly attract your prospective clients' attention and lead them from where they are to where they want to go — to show them the bridges they need to burn (the things that haven't been working for them) and then the leap they have to take to get the results they seek.

One of the things my clients have always said to me is that I *saw* them achieving their sales goals before they could even picture it. I think about that often because it's true — and it is key to selling with synchronicity. When I meet someone, I don't see them where they are today with their sales, I see them where they will be in the near future. Being successful in business and sales is about seeing the potential in individuals and businesses and then helping them get there.

Because you know the value of your products and services, it's easy for you to see how you can help someone solve their problems. But one of the keys to sales is coaching the prospect to see this with you, by helping them to identify The Gap between where they are *now* and where they *want to* or *can go*, and how your product or service can get them there.

It's about coaching your clients through The Gap. And when I say coaching, I don't mean literally coaching them.

It's about coaching your clients through The Gap.

I am talking about supporting them through the process of figuring out where they are and where you can take them. Ask them powerful questions regarding where they are now, what their challenges are, what they would like to change, and what they believe would really support them in making those changes. Once you know that, you can help them take bold inspired action.

Whether you are selling a manufactured product or a service, by the end of that conversation, you will know exactly what they need and how you can deliver it to get them results. And when you connect with them and lead them in this way, they will buy from you.

Why will they buy from you instead of from someone else?

Because they will be able to sense that you can truly solve their problem — and take them from where they *are* to where they *want to go*. I promise you, they do not want to have to go out and talk to fifty other people. Instead, they want you to be the answer. They want you to be able to solve their problem. If you are confident that you can solve their problem, they will feel it, and they will say "yes."

Staying Committed to Your Big Why and Your Clients

The more you take bold inspired action and get results, the more influence you will have. Who you are being and how you are showing up in the world matters more than you might believe. People are always watching you, all of the time, and they are hungry for leadership. They are desperate to have someone stand for something so they can stand for something.

> Who you are being and how you are showing up in the world matters more than you might believe.

It's really exciting, especially after putting time and effort (and on some occasions, sweat and tears) into solving other people's problems, to be acknowledged for your work. Yet, this is the time where I see many entrepreneurs and professionals get it wrong. In my experience, there is usually a moment where the desire to help and lead others gets blown up by the ego, and the danger is in taking the clients' power away — beginning to make decisions for them. We can convince ourselves that our intentions are good, but the moment *it* becomes all about *us*, it's no longer about leadership, and it's no longer about helping others. The key is to stay focused on your clients and the problems you solve for them.

Leading You

The easiest way to make this shift is to change the way you are being. Once you start to really take bold inspired action and lead your business and your sales goals, your confidence will grow, and how you are showing up in the world will shift.

As your journey continues to unfold, you will see the success of others and it will activate something inside of you. It will either inspire you to emulate some of their successful ideas, or it will irritate you to the point that you will either change what you are doing, or you will put your stake in the ground and decide that the path you are on is perfect for you. In any case, taking bold inspired action toward your goals will get you where you want to go!

What bold, inspired action is waiting for you?

Committed to My Big Why

by Kathy Clark

Wow. It's the end of 2012, and I can hardly believe how things have changed in just one year. I'm happy in my business, the clients are great, and the money is flowing. That little cabin may not be just a pipe dream after all. And it's all because of Ursula. She didn't give up.

I thought back to the first time I met her.

Another networking dinner. I'm getting tired of these events. I'm supposed to be meeting new clients and growing my business, but it's not happening.

I took a deep breath and walked into the ballroom, hoping that something would be different.

I need to grow my business…fast.

I sat down at the table and enjoyed conversations with the other women, but still nothing shifted in the direction of business…until the introductions started around the room. I was startled when a new member stood up and started her 30-second spot by quoting the words of Eleanor Roosevelt, "You must do the thing you think you cannot do," and talked about her mission to help entrepreneurs and sales professionals sell with intention. I immediately thought, *Well, I hate sales. I need to get to know her.*

Having struggled for almost five years to grow my business, I made the decision to get committed. I signed up for coaching.

"Alright, Kathy. Let's get started. What are your sales goals? And how are you currently marketing your business?"

It was our first coaching session, and I was both excited and nervous.

"Well, I have been developing a focus on employee benefit statements, and I have been joining various networking groups to market that service. I think I'm going to the right places, but trying to get people's attention has been tricky. They *really* need my help, and yet I seem to be unable to communicate the importance of what I can do for them." I paused, wondering if I should share my latest silly idea for getting attention. "I have actually been entertaining the thought of dressing my husband up in a statement costume and letting him talk about the benefits of the hidden paycheck."

She looked at me across the table and said, "I think that's a great idea. It's bold enough to draw some attention." I was shocked she thought it was good idea.

Who is this person? Is she serious? I guess I do have to be bold.

I continued working with Ursula, but something inside of me was unsettled. I wanted to be bold. I wanted to help people with my services. And I definitely wanted to make some money. But something still wasn't quite right. I pulled away from the coaching and watched Ursula's business grow like crazy over the next couple of years.

In 2009, Ursula offered the Quantum Leap Mastermind opportunity, and I decided to take some bold action and sign up.

I have to start making more money. We lost way too much last year with the market crash. My poor husband was utterly broken-hearted that we lost our custom-built cabin. *I have to find a way to replenish the retirement funds and maybe even buy a little cabin. But spending more money on the business? Well, I guess I have to.*

The mastermind was where the big shifts began to take place when I finally admitted out loud that I really did not like what I was doing.

"What I really wish I could do is cook for people. Seriously, I read cookbooks like novels."

Ursula smiled, obviously observing the shift in my energy as I talked about it. "I had no idea. What is possible around the cooking? Have you been thinking about a business?"

"Well, I have thought about marketing my dad's dip recipe."

"Let's see where it goes, Kathy. How can we help you with the first step?"

We talked about what was possible, and I left the meeting excited. I went home and did some research, talked to professionals in the food business, and even visited a company that produces the recipe.

However, within a few weeks, the wind had left my sails. It was going to take some serious money to get the idea off the ground.

It's not practical for me to go in this direction right now. What else can I do?

Shortly after I let the idea go, a pyramid-selling organization showed up with an opportunity to make some money. Something about it didn't feel quite right, but I couldn't put my finger on it.

I guess I still just haven't found that thing I want to do. But time is running out. I need to replenish the retirement...fast.

When I received Ursula's invitation to Sales Coach Now-LIVE 2012, I registered immediately, hoping that something would shift for me there.

Mid-morning on the first day, one of the speakers asked, "How many of you know you could make $10,000 per month?" and I noticed one of my friend's hands shoot up. I waited for a break in the program and approached her.

"I noticed you raised your hand when she asked how many people could make $10,000 per month. That's great! How are you going to do that?"

"I'm selling life insurance, and it's very promising. What are you up to these days, Kathy?"

I told her about the pyramid organization and that I wasn't terribly excited about it. She looked me straight in the eye and said, "Get out."

"I know. But what am I going to do?"

"Why don't you sell life insurance? You know benefits. You could do this. I love that I am helping people protect their futures, and I'm making good money."

That shift I was praying for happened inside of me when she said those words.

This must be my answer to my prayers! I'm doing it!

When Ursula invited me to her breakfast the next day and shared the Synchronize MasterMind opportunity with me, I knew it would be a bold way to start my new business. My friend had already given me a few connections and promised that the money could be good.

When Ursula said the investment was almost $10,000, I caught my breath.

Holy cow! That's a lot of money!

"Ursula, something is telling me to sign up." I pulled her aside after the breakfast. "I just don't know about the money. Do you think this is the right place for me? Am I ready for this?"

"Yes, I think a step this big could do a lot for you, Kathy.

It's a huge intention to set, and the results come when you take bold action. However, if you want to hold a spot, but then get home and decide it's not for you, just call me." She gave me that look — the one that quietly said, *Kathy, you deserve to do this for yourself.*

The nagging didn't go away. I can't explain it, but I just felt like I had to do it. So I did.

During one of the mastermind sessions, I was sharing how I wanted to be of service to people. The emotion bubbled up when I said the words, "I want to protect the dreams of entrepreneurs."

Everyone took a deep breath, like they had felt the impact of what I was doing for people.

And, in that moment, I felt the impact too. I felt like I was finally home — that I had finally found my passion.

I left that mastermind with inspiration, intensity, and boldness that I have never before felt in business, and I hit the ground running.

In just a few months, I had enlisted the help of an outside sales person and have just closed a really big deal for a client. I have been presented with numerous opportunities to market my business, and I have returning clients already signing up for support in 2013.

It feels so good to be in my element — serving others and making money.

Ursula was right — selling can be easy, when you've found your Big Why and put your stake in the ground to serve others.

I can't wait to see what happens next!

 **Kathy Clark** is founder and CEO of Mitchell Clark Insurance Solutions, a company dedicated to helping businesses protect assets and liabilities while limiting exposure to lawsuits. With more than 20 years of human resource management experience and a wealth of employee benefits expertise, Kathy excels at finding the perfect insurance solutions for her clients. As a business owner herself, she is keenly aware of the challenges and risks entrepreneurs face and has vowed to help other business owners protect their empires and lifelong dreams. Licensed in the State of California since 2001, Kathy is well versed in a variety of insurance products, and specializes in business continuation planning. She is a member of the Society for Human Resource Management (SHRM), Professionals in Human Resources Association (PIHRA), and the National Association of Insurance and Financial Advisors.

To connect with Kathy, visit
www.mitchellclark.com

Bringing Boldness to the Inland Empire

by Michelle Skiljan

Standing at the front of the room, I blinked back the tears as they applauded. I looked at Ursula and smiled when I saw the tears brimming in her eyes too.

She really is committed to our success.

I shifted my gaze to the faces of those attending one of Ursula's Selling with Intention Intensives.

It wasn't long ago that I was sitting in one of these seats, trying to figure out how to grow our non-profit, and now...Well, yeah! I am holding a check from the Wells Fargo Foundation for $50,000.

As I walked to the back of the room, I thought about how far I had come in such a short amount of time.

In October of 2003, I began my dream job, serving as the Founding Director of the Inland Empire Women's Business Center (IEWBC). I co-launched it with Paula Bahamon, and we worked ourselves to the bone the first year to get it off the ground. Although it was a non-profit with its first year's funding secured, we poured our blood, sweat, and tears into the program to meet the stated goals. It was the most terrifying and exhilarating year of my life.

In October of 2006, we secured a second SBA grant to launch the Coachella Valley Women's Business Center, a center that had begun as a part-time outreach of the IEWBC earlier that year. Although this center had a director, much work was to be done to get this center off the ground and meet the stated goals.

By the time I met Ursula, also in 2006, I was running tired, and so was my IEWBC colleague. We had developed a solid program but were burning ourselves out trying to do it all on our own. I don't know who urged me to ask for help, but almost as soon as they did, Ursula crossed our path, looking for a place to launch her own sales trainings.

This is a win-win, for sure! She'll have a space to facilitate her workshops, and our clients will benefit from learning about sales. And the best part about it — we don't have to do the training!

With Ursula in full support, the IEWBC quickly became a hub of small business experts providing their knowledge and experience to others.

"Michele, I'm thinking about offering a 3-day Selling with Intention Intensive. What do you think about the possibility of hosting it at the center and inviting your clients to take advantage of it?"

"I think it's a great idea. Let's do it!"

As soon as she implemented the course, I began hearing the whispers in the hallway.

"I can't believe it! I've set several appointments!"

"I know! I've already nearly closed a sale!"

"Ursula is amazing! She makes selling easy!"

I was jealous.

I want more ease in our sales. I am going to attend this class.

Finally, in the fall of 2007, I joined her for the three days and was amazed by everything she packed into the experience. I walked out of there with incredible clarity about why the IEWBC's mission (to help women — often low-income — to achieve small business success and self-sufficiency through self-employment), and my role there was so important. A new intensity and determination to stay on-course and grow the organization took over.

We are making a difference, but we can make a bigger impact. All we need is more funding.

Over the next few months, I remained intentional and intense. I focused on the priorities of the day-to-day operations and then spent the evenings and weekends moving the fundraising goal forward. I was excited, energized, and on-fire with enthusiasm.

In January, amidst a family health crisis, I received a last-minute notice regarding a funding opportunity with the Wells Fargo Foundation. I kept focused, handled the health crisis, and completed the funding proposal.

And, obviously, it happened. We received a check for $50,000, and I knew it was just the beginning.

What I didn't know was that the boldness and determination that Ursula had modeled and inspired in me would help me through one of the scariest health crisis I have ever faced. Tired of being jostled around in the system, I was ready to just give in to having a second surgery after the first had been unsuccessful. But I couldn't.

I kept searching, made phone calls, and kept asking for help until I got what I needed. The help I needed showed up when I got committed to finding a different way, and I am now healthy and whole as a result.

I determined at the start of 2012 to take myself to the next level. I made a commitment to myself to get to one event per month and grow my abilities, and Ursula's Sales Coach Now-LIVE was the first one I signed up for.

When Ursula asked me if I wanted to participate in the Synchronize MasterMind, I didn't hesitate. "YES!" This was just what I'd set my intention to do!

I am ready for the next level. We have endured a lot since the market crash of 2008, and both the center in San Bernardino and the one in Palm Desert are in need of some funds. I need to get even more serious about the fundraising this year.

By the end of the first mastermind, I had extremely clear fundraising goals that took me well outside of my comfort zone, but I also had outlined the opportunities, the steps, and the proposed dates for implementation.

As of the writing of this book, I am not done with the mastermind, but I have already hit 66% of my fundraising goals.

What else? What else can I do to fund the center and help more women become self-sufficient?

As far as I'm concerned, the sky is the limit. Our current economic impact is nearing $15 million, and we are committed to bringing true prosperity to the Inland Empire.

What's next? Well, we are hosting our first big conference this year and, thanks to Ursula, have booked a speaker who will not only help our clients, but will help us hit our fundraising goal fast.

 **Michelle Skiljan** is the Executive Director of the Inland Empire and Coachella Valley Women's Business Centers. Michelle's leadership skills, work ethic, and dedication to the Women's Business Center Programs has led to 4 million dollars of operational funds raised. Plus, she has been instrumental in leading her team to train 26,124 workshop participants, deliver business counseling for 2,756 business owners, and the generation of community economic impact of 15 million dollars.

To connect with Michelle, visit
www.iewbc.org

The Core Community Shift

*"Surround yourself with only people
who are going to lift you higher."*

Oprah Winfrey

Days later, synchronicity kicked in, and my phone rang.

"Hello?" I said tentatively.

"Hi! Is this Ursula?"

"Yes, this is she."

*"Hi, Ursula. You probably don't remember me. I heard you speak
three years ago, and I'd like to have you help me with the sales*

of my magazine. Would you be willing to help?"

"Sure!" I answered, surprised she still had my number after three years.

We chatted for a while, and then I found out that we not only shared the same book publisher, but that she had also completed a bestseller campaign for her book. Somehow, we had been in the same community and not known it.

When she shared that, my breath caught in my throat. I was so shocked I almost didn't know what to say. Should I have really been surprised? After all, wasn't I just living what I teach?

I knew this was the clear next step. So, I asked her if she would help me with my bestseller campaign.

"Of course."

Core Communities & Connections

The year 2008 was significant because we rebranded as *Sales Coach Now* (from *Potential Quest, Inc.*). Potential clients no longer asked what we do — they were clear that we offered sales coaching and training — and they knew pretty quickly whether or not they wanted to be part of our community. Moving with that momentum, I wrote *One Great Goal* that year, and my speaking engagements and events really started to pick up. We launched our first Sales Coach Now-LIVE event in 2009 and had over 100 people attend, which was a big deal for me! I didn't sell much at that event, but I at least made a profit and learned what I would do differently the next time. And, it was my first real glimpse at the core community shift I had made by getting committed to my mission to help sales professionals and entrepreneurs make a lot of money so they could give back to the organizations they care about — and live a great life. Little did I know how much that core community would continue to support me and *Sales Coach Now* over the coming years.

In January of 2009, through a series of synchronistic events, I attended a four-day event in Los Angeles. Just to attend the event cost over $3,000 plus hotel and travel costs. I dug deep to make it happen. I had already invested a lot in myself and the business with my master's degree in Psychology (over $40,000) and my NLP Coaching Certification ($3,000). However, I knew that every time I invested in myself or the business, my sales grew. (More on that concept in the next chapter!) The seminar was powerful for me because every speaker she had, from Marianne Williamson to Neale Donald Walsh, inspired and motivated me to think even bigger. I started to believe that some of my greatest dreams were really possible.

My intention for attending the event wasn't just to hear the phenomenal speakers, however. I also was very intentional about expanding my connections to grow my business. I wanted to expand my network. I just didn't know at the time that I was also expanding my core community, or the importance of that.

Feeling very inspired, I applied to be part of the mastermind group that was offered that weekend. I was thrilled to be accepted into one of the programs, and I held my breath when I told Tim how much it was going to cost: $15,000 plus travel to Vegas three times in one year. Instead of being concerned about the amount of money I wanted to spend, Tim smiled, "Well, it's probably what you need to get to the next level in your business. I know you will make the most of it." I am so grateful to have a husband who believes in me more than I do on most days.

> My intention for attending the event wasn't just to hear the phenomenal speakers.

My first mastermind was a powerful experience. The members of my group became dear friends and colleagues with whom I am still connected. They also became a part of my core community — the individuals I counted on when I was stuck or struggling. The collective mastermind and coaching pushed me to grow and the entire experience challenged me in ways I hadn't expected. Let's just say that I stretched way outside of my comfort zone!

The group was also instrumental in encouraging me to rewrite *Selling with Intention*, which I did, with a lot of help from Amanda! At the time, I didn't know how important writing a second edition of the book was going to be and where it was leading me. But I see now that I was not only able to expand the book with everything I had learned since the first edition, but that it was clearly the next step in my evolution and the growth of my core community.

A year later, I was connected with an individual who I hired to help me find corporate sponsors. The company represented authors and helped them create relationships and events with sponsors who were the best fit. Through that connection, I was given a ticket to attend Author 101 University in Los Angeles, which I've mentioned earlier in this book. I had a feeling that I was supposed to go, so I followed my hunch.

I remember sitting in the audience at Author 101 and I suddenly *knew* two things. First, I knew that I would find a new publisher for *Selling with Intention*. Second, I knew that I would speak on that stage someday. Sitting there, I asked myself, *How did I know that, and how did I get here?* Every synchronistic connection led me to the next step in my journey, and I was confident it would continue. I was building a powerful core community of synchronistic influence, and it felt like coming home.

Pivotal Core Community Moments

One of the most pivotal moments I experienced on my synchronistic journey was inviting New York Times Bestselling Author (and multi-millionaire) Loral Langemeier to speak on my stage at Sales Coach Now-LIVE 2011. I asked Loral to speak at my event October of 2010 when I met her at Author 101, and then I stressed for months until February 4 (the day of my event) arrived! Yes, I was excited to have her speak at my event, but I was even more excited to introduce her to my core community. Her message that "making money is easy" was an important conversation for me to bring them.

> She hugged me as she got on stage and whispered, "Great job! They love you!"

Loral flew in on her private jet. I connected with her briefly, and then ran back up on stage to introduce her. I remember asking everyone to get on their feet, and Brian (my AV team leader) brought the music up really loud as she ran up to the stage. As she walked toward me, I thought *Wow! I did it! We have a packed room! Loral is speaking at my event! WOOOO HOOOO!* She hugged me as she got on stage and whispered, "Great job! They love you!"

All I could say was, "Thank you for being here, Loral!"

I walked to the back of the room and sat down on a chair, so hard that I thought maybe I had broken the chair, but it was fine. I kept breathing and said a prayer, thanking God for that beautiful moment. I had sacrificed so much to get to that moment. I had worked so hard. But in that moment, I also knew I didn't want it to be "hard" anymore.

Having Loral speak at my event took my confidence and belief in myself as a speaker and entrepreneur to another level. Loral moves at 100 miles per hour, but when you have a few moments with her, she inspires you to create a new belief in yourself. She looks past your eyes and into your soul, and she sees something that you cannot. She saw that being a New York Times bestselling author is a possibility for me. She saw that speaking on national and international stages is a possibility for me. And she saw my future as a multi-millionaire. Sometimes you need someone else to believe it before you can, and she has held that space for me.

That was my second Sales Coach Now-LIVE event. And, it was by far our most profitable event ever and also the most meaningful because I could see the difference that my company was making in people's lives. Even though it had been hard to get there, I started to see that more was possible — *much more* — and I was excited to take the next synchronistic steps on my path.

The clear next step was joining Loral's mastermind group, The Big Table. I had taken her 3 Days to Cash class and won the sales contest during her event (what choice did I have?). Yes, I was investing in my business again, *and* I knew it would pay off. Plus, traveling to Tahoe with Tim every few months to attend the mastermind group seemed like a fun bonus. Loral, and her community, had become a very important part of my synchronistic core community.

Jim Rohn, one of the original thought leaders in self-development, said, "You are the average of the five people you spend the most time with." I always disliked that statistic! But there is a lot of truth to it. If you want to increase your prosperity (whatever that means for you), you need to expand your core community to include those people who are already prosperous. Why? You are *always* being influenced by the people around you, whether you are conscious of it or not.

Synchronicity happens even faster when we are consistently with a core community that challenges us to think bigger, holds intentions with us, and encourages us to leave fear behind.

I have always participated in and facilitated mastermind groups because I have wanted to work even closer with my core community. Surrounding ourselves with prosperous people on an ongoing basis is critical. In fact, synchronicity happens even faster when we are consistently with a core community that challenges us to think bigger, holds intentions with us, and encourages us to leave fear behind.

Finding Your People

I love Seth Godin's book *Tribes* because he talks about the importance of finding your people and building a core community — a tribe, as he refers to it — of followers and members:

> "A tribe is a group of people connected to one another, connected to a leader, and connected to an idea. For millions of years, human beings have been part of one tribe or another. A group needs only two things to be a tribe: a shared interest and a way to communicate... Tribes need leadership. Sometimes one person leads, sometimes more. People want connection and growth and something new. They want change... You can't have a tribe without a leader — and you can't be a leader without a tribe."

Sales Coach Now, my company, has been about building a core community and bringing like-minded people together from the start. That core community holds the intention and space for transformation to occur for all who join us on this journey.

The crazy truth is, however, you really don't find a community; they find you, and you know it when you meet them. What do I mean by that? Your core community is comprised of people like you — people who share your beliefs, values, and interests. Your core community will be drawn to you because of how you show up in the world and how they view you. The best way to grow your core community is to *just be yourself.* Yes, you read that correctly. When you are being your most authentic self, people will know whether or not they are a part of your core community pretty quickly.

Your core community is not defined by size; it can be a handful of people or thousands. Again, what matters is how they are aligned with your beliefs, values, and interests.

Finding my core community was pretty painful. What I mean by that is that we all want to belong. We want to be part of something. When I first started speaking, I thought "the speaker world" was my core community, my family, but I found out pretty quickly that it wasn't. After all, we all spoke on different topics and had varied beliefs, values, and interests, so it made sense that we didn't all connect. Yet, what I discovered is that my core community — my people — were waiting for me at the back of the room, waiting to connect, wanting to sell more in their business and give back to the organizations they cared about. When you take inspired action and become visible in the world, your core community will find you.

Remember, most of us are hungry for leadership and when we find someone to follow, we will follow them to the ends of the earth, almost to a fault. Being the leader of your core community comes with great responsibility. We've all seen examples of power abuse, scams, and poor leadership. Be careful who you follow, and who persuades you to become part of their community, because you want to make sure that they have *your* best interest in mind, not their own.

Who are the top ten people that you would like to have in your core community? What are their values, and why is it important to have them walking with you? What are the values of your target clients that make them the perfect fit to travel with you and your core community?

Mentors and Coaches

Finding a mentor or coach who has *your* best interest in mind may not be easy to do, but they are a very important part of your core community. I talk to so many people who have been jilted by their supposed mentors or coaches and feel completely left behind. If you find a mentor who really wants you to succeed, and it's not in their personal interest or an outside organization's interest, hold onto them, for they are more precious than gold.

I first heard about the importance of having a mentor in high school. You could call some of my teachers mentors, but they were my mentors for only a short period of time, then they had to focus on their next batch of students. That I completely understood. My elementary school teachers in LeCenter, Minnesota, were top notch. I was blessed to attend a small town public school, my first core community, filled with teachers who really cared about giving us the best education they could. I remember them being a close community as well, supporting each other as our classes moved from one level to the next.

My first true mentor showed up in high school. Her name was Marcia, and she was a wonderful social worker at our school that met with kids if they needed extra support. Marcia showed up exactly when I needed some extra support. We met regularly for a few years, and she's the reason I got into St. Olaf, a wonderful private Lutheran College in Northfield, Minnesota. If it wasn't for Marcia, I would not have had the courage to apply to a private school. Even though I had excellent grades, was a member of the Honor Society, and served as the senior class president, there was a part of me that didn't feel *good enough*. Marcia wrote me a letter of recommendation, so I filled out the application and was accepted. Being accepted and joining this new community was a huge leap for me. I was starting to realize that I didn't have to live within my limited expectations for myself. I could live into my potential. Looking back, I wish I would have applied to Harvard!

Great mentors see things in you that you don't see. They see your potential. Not for personal gain, but because they want you to live up to what's possible for YOU. And they are a critical part of your core community and growth.

Great mentors see things in you that you don't see.

Look around your life. Who has mentored you? Who might be considered a mentor you need to seek out?

Develop Meaningful Partnerships

Finding meaningful joint venture and strategic partners who share your target client database can help you significantly grow your sales in a short amount of time. The key, though, is to be sure that their values are in alignment with yours. Always trust your gut because the last thing you want to do is partner up with someone who doesn't share your beliefs, values, or interests (your core community). These types of partnerships will most certainly lead to problems.

I attended a seminar on partnering a few months ago, and it was very eye opening for me. The speaker talked about the importance of partners and how to ensure that they would be a good fit for you. He took us through an exercise to determine some of the potential partners who were already in our circle of influence, or our core community. I thought of one immediately who I had already been doing some partnering with. The speaker's question was to have us think about either initial (if it was a new partner) or additional ways that we could partner (for existing partners). A powerful idea flashed into my head, and I wrote it down. He then asked how much money this partnership could lead to, and I wrote down $100,000.

Six figures.

Here's where the magic came in. I didn't do anything else. I had only written it down and was thinking how great it would be, and then I forgot about it. About two weeks later, I received a text from that exact partner proposing a new way that we might be able to work together. It was exactly the idea I had been thinking of — but even better.

Ah, the power of synchronicity!

So who do you want to play with in your core community?

My Paul McCartney Moment

On a gorgeous Tuesday morning in 2010, I was given a very "loud" message about the impact of synchronicity on our core communities. There I was, enjoying a birthday tea party for two of my dear friends. We were sipping tea, laughing, and enjoying our time together when suddenly we heard loud pounding outside. I looked out the window and saw my neighbor talking to a man who was laughing loudly with her and pounding his hand on the big gray electrical box at the end of my driveway. I thought it was a friend of hers, so I sat back down at the table, glad that everything was okay.

A few minutes later, the doorbell rang. It rang twice in two loud bursts, so I knew it was my neighbor (she always rang our doorbell like that), but I had no idea what she wanted. I opened the door, expecting to see her, but instead saw the gentleman she had been speaking with outside.

"Hi," he started, "My name is Mike (not his real name) and, well, wow, this is quite a moment for me. I cannot believe that I am standing here talking to *you!* You have no idea, no idea how I got here! I can't believe it! This is like meeting Paul McCartney!"

There are a few moments in life that make you really pause…and laugh out loud! This was one of those moments for me. I could hear my friends laughing behind me (you know, the friends who *really* know you and keep you grounded). I tried to process what Mike was saying as my head started to get a little cloudy. What did he mean by saying that meeting me was like meeting Paul McCartney? Who was this guy?

And more importantly, how did I get to the point where someone would actually think that meeting me was a big deal to them? That perhaps I had some information or knowledge that could make their life easier? I decided then and there that something really important had just happened to me — something that I was going to need to

> How did I get to the point where someone would actually think that meeting me was a big deal to them?

share with others who could benefit from this moment…my Paul McCartney Moment.

First, I wanted to figure out why this was such a big deal to Mike. He explained that he had been looking for help with his sales, and he happened to come across one of my YouTube videos. *(Really? People watch my YouTube videos?)* Then, out of the blue, he happened to mention me to someone, and they knew me, which felt like a very big coincidence to him — a synchronistic moment for him, right? Mike owns a landscaping business, and one day he went to cut the lawn of a new client. Somehow my name came up again and the woman he was telling started to laugh. She said, "Ursula is my next door neighbor!"

That is how he ended up knocking on my door. And to this day, he's still part of my core community and really values what I teach.

The point is, remember that *you* are Paul McCartney to someone. You may not realize that yet. You might not get it. But it is not a coincidence that you are reading this book. There are many "Mike's and Mary's" who are just waiting to be a part of your core community. And as your core community grows, so will your business.

Have Fun & Make It a Bestseller

by Jenée Dana

"What?!? What do you mean you *lost* the inventory order I sent three weeks ago? I am running the campaign right now!" It took everything I had not to scream obscenities at the poor soul on the other side of the phone who really had no control of the situation. I hung up when they said there was nothing more they could do.

Are you freakin' kidding me?!? Two years of work, leading up to this moment, down the f@#$ing drain? Shaking with a combination of rage and fear, I picked up the phone and called my book coach Amanda.

I don't think she understood more than 25% of what I said I was crying so hard, but she calmed me down. "Jenée, I can't imagine that all of the synchronicity that has

187

happened for the last two years has been for this moment to fall apart. I have never seen so much ease and synchronicity happen for someone on this path (except for maybe Ursula). Take a deep breath and remember how it felt to see everything fall together for you. That can happen again here. You've got this. Now, who can we call to fix this problem?"

She was right. The last two years had been amazing — full of synchronistic connections that I could hardly believe as they were happening — and it all started when I met Ursula.

I was only seven months into the brand new company I had co-founded, and I was excited and scared. You know that feeling you have right before the rollercoaster takes off at the theme park? You feel like you might throw up, but it doesn't matter because the ride is worth it? That's exactly how it felt to set out in business at the ripe age of twenty-five.

I began attending networking meetings and conferences, looking for people to connect with — people who would understand me and be able to help me. But the circles I went to weren't what I had hoped they would be.

When I met Ursula, I knew I had to work with her. Among some of the entrepreneurs I had met, she was one of the special few who didn't turn their nose up at me and treat me like a kid, "How old are you? You look like you are in high school. What do you do?" Instead, she immediately saw my gifts and potential, and offered her help.

Little did I know what was going to come out of that one offer. I immediately found myself surrounded by other like-minded entrepreneurs who had tremendous gifts that would not only support me in making my dreams happen, but that would demonstrate the power of synchronicity and community.

The first connection made was with Amanda. I knew I wanted to write a book, but I had no idea what it would look like. I had a few ideas, but at Amanda's first meeting, I got the clarity I needed when she asked me the simple question: "Well, where did you acquire all of your productivity skills and strategies?"

"Hmm, I graduated UCLA in three years, after spending the first two years hating life." The small group was silent, and I waited for them to respond.

"So, what if you wrote a book to show young people how to do that? It would be easier for you to establish credibility there than with the market you've been pursuing. You can write the other one later."

I felt the shift happen inside of me, and in one of the following masterminds, my brand revealed itself: "Have Fun & Get It Done." That's what I am all about, and Ursula's community had helped me to see myself and my value in a powerful new way. Pretty soon, I was letting go of "the mold" I thought I had to fit into, which meant that I started showing up to networking events in my stylish jeans, cute blouses, and hot high heels, instead of those awful business suits. I was a little scared at first, but it didn't take long for me to realize that I was getting better reactions and results.

Yes! I found the right crowd! I can feel comfortable in my own skin around them.

The world of possibilities started to open up to me, and I just went with it. I started dreaming about hitting #1 on the bestseller list, and I knew that in order to do that, I had to have amazing content, incredible design, and community support. The content was easy with Amanda's help, and then I was synchronistically connected through my new community with graphic designers Dan Mulhern and Dawn Teagarden. They were both so excited to support me.

Then I was gifted a ticket to a marketing bootcamp, where I started telling everyone I met that I was writing a book. I made some incredible connections, but when I heard two of the speakers, actors Glenn Moreshower (actor on hit series 24 and blockbuster Transformers) and Richard

Hatch (Apollo in original Battlestar Galactica), I knew I wanted their stories in my book. I took a deep breath and asked them. They both agreed happily, gave me their information, and said they looked forward to our conversation.

For real? It's this easy?

When Amanda and I were discussing exercises to include in the book, I told her I really wanted to include Smart Cookies' Perfect Day Exercise. She agreed that it was a good idea if I could get their permission.

Uggh, what are the chances of that?

I was shocked when they responded to my email in less than fifteen minutes. They asked to look at the book and then they not only gave me permission to use the exercise, they gave me a phenomenal endorsement. I did an embarrassing happy dance in my office.

And then it was time…time to share with Ursula and my mastermind that I was ready to hit #1 on the bestseller list. She smiled and started talking strategy, and I was able to learn a ton from her during her own campaign. I volunteered to help in any way I could, and she gave me some really amazing tips.

I put everything into motion for the campaign and, only a few weeks later, found out that I was moving to Hawaii with my fiancé on a job transfer.

Great googly moogly! How am I going to run a campaign from Hawaii?!? The population is so small, I don't know anyone there, and…

And then I had to laugh! There I was freaking out about how I was going to do something when I had just proven the power of intention and synchronicity.

It's only been a month since I did that visualization about moving to Hawaii. And it showed up already? But really, how am I going to do this?

Ursula's response was so matter-of-fact: "Why couldn't you run the campaign from Hawaii? It could all be done virtually. What about those student organizations that need your book? Have you contacted them?" We talked out the details for a few minutes, and as soon as she got off the phone, she sent an email with several contacts that she thought would be a good fit. When I opened the email, I felt the shift happen again.

Goodbye, fear and scarcity. I am going to kick this campaign's ass!

Everything went as planned…until they lost my inventory order — the day of the bestseller campaign.

I did the only thing I knew to do and reached out to the core community that had helped me get this far. Ursula, Amanda, and others reminded me of my ability to attract synchronicity and step into the flow. And that's what I did.

I am hitting #1 amazon bestseller because I am enough and I deserve it...this is happening!

I clicked over to the Amazon screen and saw my book hit #13 (my lucky number) and my belief shifted deeper.

#1 is within reach. There wasn't any doubt. *I got this!*

When my book hit #1 on Amazon in the first category, I hit the roof. Some joyous obscenities flew out of my mouth, I did another embarrassing happy dance, screamed, ran around the house like a crazy person, and then called my fiancé, my mom, Ursula, my book coach, and everyone else I know to share the good news!

A few months later, the momentum from the campaign was fizzling, and I decided I wanted the book to win an award. But how? I researched online and found some of the most reputable reviewers and book awards that allowed self-published authors to enter with the 'Big Boys.' I found Readers' Favorite Book International Awards, and my pulse started racing.

Should I even apply? What if they hate it and give me a bad review?

And then I remembered what Ursula taught me about setting the intention and anchoring a good feeling to it. I did it. I saw myself entering and winning the award, and then I completed the application.

As this book is being completed, I am on my way to Florida to accept my GOLD MEDAL AWARD with other amazing authors like Sheri Fink, Paul Michael Glaser (the original Starsky in "Starsky and Hutch") and more.

It's amazing what can happen when you surround yourself with a core community of people who care about your goals as much as you do.

 **Jenée Dana** graduated UCLA in 3 years and still had a blast, in spite of struggling with ADHD and undiagnosed reading disabilities. Completing the final two years of the UCLA academic requirements in one, while working to help cover her living expenses, Jenée had more fun than she had in her first two years. After combining the best productivity tools she could find, she watched her grades go up, her social life become more fun, and her single parent mom sigh with relief to save a year of tuition. Today, as the President and Chief Focusing Officer of **www.MyFocusBook.com** and award-winning, bestselling author of *Have Fun & Get It Done*, Jenée helps young people and entrepreneurs and professionals increase their productivity and their fun factor! She lives in Hawaii with her fiancé.

To connect with Jenée, visit
www.myfocusbook.com

And the Beat Goes On...Fast

by John Zahn

You never know when, or how, synchronicity may strike, but it does.

The crowd was bigger than I expected, and I was thrilled that we had decided to host a ribbon cutting with the Seal Beach Chamber of Commerce to celebrate our membership. It wasn't just a chance for Omnibeat to invite members to see our cool digs, it had given us a serious deadline to have our place and promotional materials ready to go. I had high hopes for this launch, but knew it could take some time to get some traction.

One step at a time.

197

After some food, drinks, and a brief presentation of what Omnibeat is about, I cut the ribbon. As the people began to disperse, a man approached me and introduced himself as the husband of one of the members and a local graphic designer. "John, I am really impressed with your whole brand. You guys are up to great things, and I want to introduce you to a company that needs your help. I've been working on their design, but they desperately need someone to help them build a presence online." He told me the name of the company, and I took a deep breath to contain my excitement.

Penta Water? That's a national brand! This is the break we've been looking for — a nice big feather in the cap!

My core community was working its magic. He agreed to make the connection, and I thanked him and promised to follow up immediately.

As I cleaned up and prepared to go home, I wondered if I would have been prepared for such a huge opportunity if not for Ursula.

I can recognize the synchronicity. Funny how synchronicity put me in her space at just the right time...

The morning was full of activity, as usual. I was rushing to another networking breakfast, hoping that I hadn't missed a stain on my shirt, and that I might meet some potential clients and strategic partners.

I hope they have a good speaker today. Sometimes — rarely — they are terrific, but most often they are pitching ideas that just aren't me. It took a bit of effort to get in that open frame of mind to allow new thoughts in.

When I saw the topic was *Selling with Intention*, I thought, *Well, I'm a natural born and raised salesman, so this can't be too bad.*

It turned out to be one of the best presentations I've ever heard on sales, and I realized as she spoke how dormant my thoughts about sales had been.

I've been too busy running around and putting out fires to really focus on selling with intention.

It brought me back to college, and even before my stepfather, one of the world's best salesmen, taught me the ropes.

These are great tools and innovative ideas, and she is a powerful woman. I had no idea that in a short period of time, Ursula would make such a great impression on me and awaken the sleeping sales giant within me.

I love people, and I love putting deals together.

I listened very carefully and wrote notes as she went along. She inspired me to want to succeed, "Double your sales in 60 days! Set a goal and stretch for even more."

A core community shift had occurred, and I knew that this woman was most likely going to become an integral part of my future success. I've wanted something like this to happen, but I wasn't sure what or who I was looking for.

I knew that something great was out there. I could feel it, and now I see it.

Ursula was just what I needed to help clear away the clutter and focus on the most important thing — selling with intention!

I've always known that surrounding myself with smart and capable people brings me closer to the next level, and I've always found myself in communities, working hard to make those connections.

Two years before I met Ursula, I had a business coach who took me through a series of typical exercises to figure out how to grow my business.

Blah, blah, blah, sell more pools to get where you want to be in ten years. The real problem that presented itself was that the number of pools I would have to sell was darn near impossible. A light went on.

This business is not the right vehicle to get me where I want to be. Wow, all this work and coaching, and I'm nowhere!

And then I had met Nate — a real whipper-snapper of a kid — through Rotary Club. Nate is a computer grad from CSULB, and I put him to work on my website. He impressed me and then encouraged me to use social media to market the business. "Go for it," I told him.

I certainly don't know how to use it!

He worked his magic, and my revenue soared while others were suffering or worse.

Aha! Maybe Nate and I can help others achieve this type of success!

Omnibeat was born.

Wikipedia, the all-knowing online encyclopedia, says synchronicity is the experience of two or more events that appear to be casually unrelated or unlikely to occur together by chance, yet are experienced as occurring together in a meaningful manner.

Synchronicity was definitely at work here. In a span of a few months, a coach helped me see that I needed a new vehicle, and I met a young man that exposed me to that new vehicle. We worked together and laid a good foundation for the business, but there were doubts and times when I wondered whether or not it was really synchronicity at work. And then I met Ursula, who helped me to make the big shift happen and begin to fulfill my dream over the course of her 60-day program. She helped me to step back into synchronicity and quickly expand my core community again.

When the program was over, I reached out to her, "Ursula, I am so excited about everything that has happened since I met you. I landed a big client, my revenue is steadily growing, I've been taking more family vacations, and life is getting better and better. I don't want it to stop. What's next?"

She chuckled and started asking questions. I was impressed that Ursula really wanted to hear about my story with all of the details. As she shares in her book, selling isn't telling — it is asking questions so you can help.

I paced around the backyard of one of the coolest pools I have ever built, with my mind racing. All I could think about was how Omnibeat was ready to be catapulted into orbit and how this woman could help me get it there. I got it! This MasterMind is very intensive with direct interaction with Ursula and her team.

I'm in! I need this type of accountability, and I want to know more about these "synchronistic shifts" she keeps talking about. I was sold before she even asked me if I thought it was the right direction for me.

When I heard the date of the first meeting, I was terribly disappointed. I had already planned a trip with my wife to Seattle and Vancouver BC. "How could this work if I miss the first event?" Ursula responded immediately that she would personally meet with me at my office to get me up to speed so I could be a part of the mastermind group. It gave me an overwhelming feeling of commitment that this is what I needed.

It is going to work!

Success is a formula of doing the right things every day. I know this, yet it is easy to get side-tracked with life, health, family, work, and so on. Ursula has helped me to reset my formula to actively make more connections within my core community. The more effort in, the more effort out. She really makes it simple. Selling with intention is *not* about me; it's about helping those within our circles. It becomes contagious!

In fact, as I was finishing this chapter, the marketing director at Penta Water called me and confirmed that these synchronistic questions are going to continue:

"John, I can't believe it. Two emails, and we made more than $20,000. Amazing!"

"Yeah, and we're just getting started." The confidence oozed out of me.

"Well, I'm going to connect you with our marketing agency director today, so that you can help them out too."

"Thank you for the connection. I will be sure to follow up."

Wow! Another national brand in just a few months! What's next?

After more than twenty years of being a small business owner and working hard to create presence for his companies, **John Zahn** decided to go online with the help of a tech-savvy young man named Nate Trimmer. Embracing these technologies allowed John to dramatically increase his visibility, his credibility, and his revenue. In just six months, John grew his business by 20%. Excited to help others find the same success, he joined forces with Nate to create Omnibeat and is inspiring others to share their unique story and grow their businesses quickly and easily with a powerful online presence.

To connect with John, visit
www.omnibeat.com

The Money Shift

*"If you want one year of prosperity, plant corn.
If you want ten years of prosperity, plant trees.
If you want one hundred years of
prosperity, educate people."*

Unknown

I remember the first time I realized that most bestseller campaigns, even *New York Times* bestseller campaigns, were driven by powerful marketing campaigns. I always thought they happened because people naturally sold a lot of books. Well, that DOES happen for some people. Just not for most.

My belief, though, was that bestseller campaigns were expensive and you had to hire a company to do it for you. Plus, you would *have to pay between $10,000 and $35,000 for the campaign. Whew! I didn't believe I had THAT kind of money.*

"Well, I wonder if there is an easier way? A faster way?" I pondered to myself.

I decided to take my own teaching and turn it on myself. I always tell my clients to ask themselves, "What is the fastest and easiest way to reach your sales goal?" When they ask that question, the ideas just start to flow.

"What is the fastest and easiest way to design a bestseller campaign?" The answer to that question was so clear, so easy, but it required me to go outside my comfort zone and ask my core community to purchase multiple copies of my books. But when they asked me, "Why not ask us to purchase ten, fifteen or twenty?" I was forced to look at why I hadn't asked for more in the first place.

So I shifted my belief and allowed myself to ask for help. I asked people to purchase multiple copies, and I was shocked by how many people came forward to get involved with the campaign.

The Big Table

In 2010, I attended Loral Langemeier's 3 Days to Cash course. I was excited to go, but the timing was terrible, as we were only one week out from my second annual Sales Coach Now-LIVE event where Loral would also be speaking. Luckily, we had been selling and promoting the event for months, and we had almost two hundred people registered by the time the 3 Days to Cash class rolled around. And yet, I understand "no-show" rates and that, like the airlines, we needed to overbook the event to ensure a full room.

With this intention, I decided I would simply sell Sales Coach Now-LIVE at 3 Days to Cash and continue to fill the event while I was there. When I arrived, I found out there would be a sales contest. This caused some anxiety because I knew that I'd have to win if I was to retain my "Sales Expert" status, especially considering that Loral would be speaking at my event the following week! On the other hand, the sales contest was exactly what I needed to overbook my event. I set my intention to win.

Throughout the three days, we had a few updates regarding how everyone was doing in terms of their sales goals. Most people were struggling, and I found myself helping them whenever I could. I also bought a lot of stuff that weekend! On the third day, when Loral announced the winners, I was thrilled to learn that I had won in the volume category.

Going into Loral's class, I kind of knew that I was going to sign up for her mastermind. I just hadn't really admitted it to myself or my husband. I had alluded to Tim that I might, and I remember a little cloud moving across his face as he realized that I might be signing up for yet another

> The money shift is about pushing outside of your belief zone about money, especially your relationship with money.

class — and spending yet another $10,000 or more. And yes, the day I texted him for his blessing, there was a long pause. I wanted to call him, but I was still in the middle of selling and attempting to win the sales contest, which he also knew I needed to do. He finally sent his blessing back, and I let out a big sigh. While I do not need my husband's permission to do everything, we do have a rule when it comes to certain amounts of money — we both need to be in on the agreement. Loral's Big Table exceeded that amount.

The money shift is about pushing outside of your belief zone about money, especially your relationship with money. How willing you are to invest in yourself and your business will tell you a lot about where you stand in that relationship.

Investing in other high-end programs, products, or services will allow you to test whether or not you are ready to sell your own high-end products or services. If you aren't willing to invest in a high-end products or services for yourself, then you probably aren't ready to sell them. Whenever I have taken large leaps in investing in myself and my business, I have also taken large leaps in terms of the amount of the services I felt good about selling and what I charged for them.

After I signed up and the initial excitement of it wore off, I wondered what in the heck I was doing. Was this yet another synchronistic step, or a cog in my wheel? Yet, having Loral speak on my stage at Sales Coach Now-LIVE reinforced that it was the right thing to do. We had a blast sharing the stage and the day together, and I grew just being around her and watching how she made decisions and how she thought about business.

Two months later, we went to Tahoe for the first Big Table. Tim and I drove his truck up the back way (highway 395), and it was gorgeous! Snow covered the mountains, and the sun shone brightly. It was exactly what we needed. It was our first time in Tahoe, and I believe it is one of the most breathtaking places on earth. I completely understand why Loral planted her roots there (not to mention the tax savings in Nevada!). On our way up, I listened to the CDs Loral had given out to prepare us for the program. I was excited because I knew we weren't just focusing on the business, we were focusing on overall wealth and what we wanted to create in our lives. Although Tim wasn't directly participating, my business plan included our plans as a couple.

We stayed at an adorable bed and breakfast beneath massive evergreens next to large piles of fluffy snow. The owners were terrific, and they openly shared the main

cabin, hosting wine tastings with delicious cheese plates —
and their homemade waffles were out of this world. I think
Tim ate at least five a day!

Feeling nervous the first time I walked into Live Out
Loud, Loral's headquarters, I reminded myself that being
nervous was normal, since I was once again living outside
of my comfort zone. I had pretty high expectations
regarding what was going to come out of our two days
together, and I wasn't disappointed. I left with a powerful
120-day plan and a new mastermind group that I was going
to be meeting with weekly for accountability purposes.

I knew my investment in myself was going to yield some
big returns.

Money is Just Energy

Some people estimate that only 4% of all of the money
in the world is actually in physical form. The rest is
held electronically in checking, savings, retirement, and
other accounts. Considering that there is very little money
just *lying around*, it is surprising that we have such strange
beliefs about money.

In the United States of America, most people struggle with
beliefs in scarcity. As a country of immigrants, perhaps
beliefs and fears about scarcity were passed down from
generation to generation. Coming out of the last great

"repression" (recession + depression), many of those beliefs were strengthened for people. The belief that there isn't enough money just isn't true; however, people's beliefs hold that thought to be truth.

Over the years, I have read tons of books on manifesting more money, primarily because that is what I teach my clients how to do, and it is something I am very passionate about because it is tied directly to my mission. And what I've discovered is that it's not difficult to create money when you expand your beliefs about how much you want to make and what's possible for you.

Growing up on the farm, we didn't have a lot of money. Yet looking back, we were very prosperous in terms of the food we grew and the fact that my parents had little or no debt and they owned a lot of land. My experience with physical money was extremely limited though, and somehow I created a belief that you have to work hard physically to make a lot of money. I didn't under-

> My beliefs were that there wasn't enough money, I had to work really hard for it, and I could never stop working that hard because if I did, the money would stop coming.

stand the "big picture" of all of the wealth we actually had on the farm, and the belief that I created did not serve me well as I took on my first career in sales. My beliefs were that there wasn't enough money, I had to work really hard for it, and I could never stop working that hard because if I did, the money would stop coming.

When I attended the NLP-Institute of California, I learned a lot about our beliefs about money, how they were formed, and how they get in the way of our success. Beliefs are just thoughts that we repeatedly focus on and look for evidence to prove that they are true. In other words, when it comes to money, if you believe that there isn't enough, you will look for the evidence that there isn't enough in the form of bills and more bills. When you shift that belief about money and truly believe that there is more than enough, you will focus on the evidence that there are more checks coming in, or more clients, and then you will continue to look for and be aware of more opportunities. I can tell you from my own personal experience that this is true.

During the last great "repression" over the past few years, my husband and I lost a lot of money in real estate and a separate business venture. In fact, we almost lost everything that we had. We had to make quick changes, and we had to challenge all of our beliefs about money to dig out of that hole quickly. I was talking with one of my dear friends one day and she said, "Ursula, even though you are going through very difficult financial times right now, you don't show it. In fact, you are grace under pressure."

Why was I able to maintain my composure in the midst of so much stress? Because I chose to shift my focus to what was coming, not what *was*. If I had focused on losing so much money, I would have lost my mind. Instead, within a year — without filing for bankruptcy — we paid off almost $100,000 in debt, mostly to investors due to real estate deals that had gone bad. Was it easy? No. But because I stayed focused on the future, and the money that I knew was coming, we slowly climbed our way out.

Another thing that helped me stay focused on paying the money off came from Access Consciousness. They teach that instead of calling it "debt," refer to it as "past expenditures." Why? Because when you say past expenditures, it allows you to take responsibility for the money that you spend. YOU made the decisions or took the risks. It is not about blaming yourself; it is about accepting responsibility. When you take responsibility for creating past expenditures, you can take responsibility for creating money as well. Isn't that powerful? So much about creating money is about responsibility and managing your thoughts. The way in which you focus on money creates or prevents it from getting to you. Which will you choose?

Remember, money is trying to get to you. The question is, How are you blocking it? What do you need to shift to let it in?

Expand Your Plan

I have been speaking full-time since 2005. Everywhere I go, I share the principles of *Selling with Intention*, hoping that those who hear me will be inspired to take action and implement the principles that I teach so they can enjoy a fruitful sales career or profitable business.

One of the biggest problems that I see over and over again is *very small thinking*. Most entrepreneurs and sales professionals do not ask for more than they "think" they can sell. The sales goals that we set are often tiny — and not even worthy of all of the effort we are putting in.

Recently, I was coaching a client, and she shared with me that she didn't feel good about the new package that she had created. She couldn't seem to connect the value with the price. So, I had her create a list of the top ten benefits that clients would receive when they purchase that package.

I met with her after she completed the exercise, and as we were talking, I could still feel that she wasn't excited about selling her package. Then, I had a hunch. Because I am learning to just *go* with those hunches, I asked a bold question, "What if your package (the exact same package) was $5,000? How would you feel about it then?" I know this will sound crazy, but it was ten times MORE than what she was charging.

Her entire face changed. She suddenly looked happier, lighter. And then she admitted that the new price, charging ten times *more* actually felt better. In an instant, she had expanded what was possible for her. She had expanded her plan, and suddenly had prices that were more in alignment with *her* value and the value she is bringing to her clients.

Is this true for everyone? No. Sometimes people are overpriced. More times than not, though, I find that people, in the service industry especially, are underpriced. When they expand their pricing so it is in alignment with how they are showing up in the world, their sales dramatically increase.

Expanding your plan doesn't come without effort. It takes work to become great at what you do and to be able to solve your clients' problems. However, the better you become, the more your sales plan can expand, and the more money you will make. The key is to have a sales goal that is worthy of you.

Expanding your plan also requires that you increase your sales projections and effectively use a tool to track your sales pipeline.

> The key is to have a sales goal that is worthy of you.

Ready to do it?

First, you have to set a Quantum Sales Goal. You can create that by writing down your original goal for the year. Then double it, and then triple it. Now, look back at your original goal. How does it look? Small? What has changed? Nothing — merely your perspective on what's possible. You have successfully started to expand your plan.

Next, create your projections by working backwards from your Quantum Sales Goal. Doing that allows you to project your expected sales as well as your expenditures. This is a great way to stay on track and figure out how much you will be paying yourself as well as how much profit you will bring in. Next, create a budget for your business. How will you spend the money (in addition to your business expenses)? Tithing/Giving? Insurance? Savings? Vacations? etc.

Third, you cannot grow your sales if you do not know what is in your pipeline. Either use a Customer Relationship Management tool to track your sales (remember, garbage in, garbage out) or create a simple Excel Spreadsheet to track Prospects, 99% closed and Closed Sales. If they are a "Prospect," you haven't met with them yet but they meet all of your criteria for a target client. "99% closed" means that you have met with a prospect, but they haven't signed up for your product or service yet. "Closed" means you have received their payment for your product or service. Our clients use our Work in Progress Report that easily tracks those three areas. We include more extensive information about the Work in Progress Report in *Selling with Intention*.

Finally, I recommend that you add tithing (or giving, or whatever you call it) to your plan. There are many books written about the power of tithing 10% of your gross sales to your church or charities that you care about. Remember, my mission is to help entrepreneurs and sales professionals make a lot of money so they can live a great life and give back to their favorite charities. Giving back is a very important part of *Selling with Synchronicity* because it gets the money moving in your business. Why? Because when you give, you have a belief that more money is on the way, or you'd never be able to part with it. It is a powerful way to shift the flow of money in your business and is a powerful way to expand your plan.

One of my clients grew a multi-million dollar business over a very short amount of time. When I asked him how he did it so quickly, he said he had a solid plan. But his plan wasn't just about bringing in sales; it included how he would spend the money as it came in. He had plans on how to spend it in his business, marketing, sales, personally, and also how he would tithe. It was a very clear plan. He summed it up powerfully before we parted, "When I am a good steward with my money, God gives me more." Brilliant.

My encouragement to you is to do it now. Don't wait to expand the flow of money in your business! Napoleon Hill once said,

> "Do it now! It can affect every phase of your life. It can help you do the things you should do but don't feel like doing. It can keep you from procrastinating when an unpleasant duty faces you. But it can also help you do those things that you want to do. It helps you seize those precious moments that, if lost, may never be retrieved."

What are three things that you could take action on today?

Receiving

The first time someone paid me in full for our Synchronize MasterMind program, I realized that not only was I in alignment with my pricing, but that I had also built up my "receiving muscle." If we want to be successful in business, we need to be powerful receivers as well as powerful givers. I like to think of the flow of giving and receiving as an infinity symbol, or the number 8 on its side. An infinity symbol means that something is endless — it goes on forever. *Selling with Synchronicity* is best represented by an infinity symbol because it represents the flow of giving great service or products and receiving great amounts of money.

Receiving is also about learning. When I step into some-one's classroom, I take off my coach and trainer hat, and leave them at the door. I know I have a lot to learn. I know I don't know everything, and I am open to receiving whatever they are willing to share. I am a sponge.

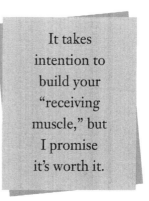

It takes intention to build your "receiving muscle," but I promise it's worth it. In fact, in my experience, the people who have a hard time receiving money (or even compliments) really struggle to grow their sales.

A Guided Money Visualization

As an NLP Certified Coach, one of the most valuable tools that I help my clients with is the power of visualization. When you work backwards from your quantum goal, your brain kicks in to fill in the gaps.

For example, let's say that your goal in the next 60 days is $20,000, or $10,000 per month. You've been averaging $5,000 per month, so this new quantum goal means that you will double your sales.

Now, think of your quantum goal. Write it down. Then, how much have you been averaging in the past three months? Now you can see where you've been, where you want to go, and the gap in between.

Next, get comfortable in your favorite chair.

> Note: You might want to have someone read this to you so you can keep your eyes closed during the entire visualization. Download and listen to this visualization for FREE when you get 30 days FREE on **www.mysalescoachnow.com**

Close your eyes. Roll your shoulders back by raising them toward your ears and back. Take a deep breath in through your nose and out through your mouth. Do that a couple more times.

Then, imagine that it is 60 days in the future, and you have achieved your quantum goal. Imagine that you are in the moment, sitting in front of your laptop, looking at your bank account online. See the total amount of your quantum goal in your bank account. As you are looking at your bank account, notice the sounds that you hear around you in your office, the scents that you smell, and the colors that you see around you. Allow all of your senses to be engaged. Then, even more importantly, notice what it feels like in your core, in your stomach area, to achieve this goal. Perhaps it is a feeling of success, confidence, or peace — whatever it is, multiply that feeling by 10 and make it reach way out to the world. As you breathe in this great feeling, put both of your hands on your heart, and anchor that feeling, knowing that you can come back to it at any time.

Keeping both hands on your heart, imagine a timeline that goes all the way back to the original date that you did the visualization. From the original date to the 60 days later when you achieved your quantum goal, notice the first two steps that you took to reach your quantum goal. Then, on that timeline, notice the limiting beliefs, fears, prospects, clients and relationships that you let go of to make room for your new clients and opportunities to show up.

Again, imagine you are sitting in your office, looking at your bank account online, imagining that you have achieved your quantum goal. Breathe in that feeling of success again and breathe out through your mouth. Trust that it is on its way.

The first time I did this exercise myself, I visualized $20,000 in my business account, and that seemed like a huge stretch for me. But I held that picture of my bank account in my mind, really believing that it was possible.

A few months later, that visualization came true. I remember opening up my bank account online and shrieking when I saw the money in my account. It was a surreal moment that reminded me anything was possible, and that if I could do it, anyone could do it.

Shifting your beliefs is just the beginning of expanding your money vision. I really want you to know that it is more than possible for you to reach your sales goals! Work on releasing your money beliefs and expanding your plan so you can live the life that you've been dreaming of.

Aligning My Pricing with My Value

by Wanda Allen

I hung up from the 60-Day Sales Success Intensive call and pondered the topic. Be intentional before every sales call. Ursula said to visualize the outcome and ask for what I wanted.

It had been almost a year since I'd given much time to my greeting card business. I'd been so preoccupied with the launch of my speaking business and book release, that I hadn't had time to do much else. *It's time to start making some card sales again.*

I had two demos scheduled. Before each one, I sat in my car, visualized the outcome, and set my intention to leave the appointments with each prospect signing up at the top level.

I walked out of both appointments with new customers at the top level. I was stunned.

Did that just happen?

It really does work. Instead of "Let me think it over," or "I'll get back to you," I heard, "Sign me up at the top level." It was the most intentional I'd ever been, and it happened exactly the way Ursula said it would.

The gratitude overwhelmed me as I reflected on the different ways she'd come in and out of my life and the crucial role she played. I would not be where I am today without her. She has been a mentor, coach, and friend since that first meeting.

After being in banking for twenty-four years, I had just learned that the bank was for sale and made the decision to become an entrepreneur — to move from being a *user* of a greeting cards program to a *distributor*. I'd developed a real passion for following up and strengthening my relationships with thoughtful notes.

Distributing — yes, I could really enjoy that!

At my first networking luncheon as an entrepreneur, I struggled with my new role.

I'm here, with no bank name or big title backing me up. Just Wanda Allen, Greeting Card Distributor.

I fumbled through the handouts at the table and noticed her name: Ursula Mentjes, Keynote Speaker, Author of *Selling with Intention.*

After her presentation, I decided to purchase her book. She offered to sign it, and asked, "What do you do, Wanda?" I told her about the bank merger and my career change.

"That's great. You'll love entrepreneurship. What's your monthly sales goal?"

I made up my answer. "Six new customers per month." Having pulled the number out of the air, I stumbled when she asked the next question: "What's your closing ratio, and how many calls/demos will it take to hit your monthly goal?" My answer, full of *uh's* and *um's*, left me feeling embarrassed.

She graciously said goodbye, and I left.

I need an action plan for my sales goals. Sitting in my car, I looked at her book and remembered she signed it. Opening it up, I saw the question, "What's the next thing for you to do?"

Three months later, I received an invitation to Ursula's 3-day Selling with Intention class and signed up without hesitation. It was phenomenal, and I was so excited to get home and implement what I'd learned.

It all worked! I subsequently received two promotions with the greeting card company, and consistently hit my monthly sales goals.

After hearing numerous compliments on my follow-up practices, "You're so good at follow-up. You always stay in touch. You never forget my birthday. You provide great customer service." I wondered if I should start speaking on the subject of follow-up. The idea wouldn't leave me alone, so I decided to do it.

As I began speaking to networking groups and business organizations, I was stunned by the response and the fact that, in general, many people fall short in the area of follow-up. The feedback motivated me to expand my speaking business by creating a workshop designed for sales teams *and* writing a book.

Three months after starting my speaking business, I received an invitation to Ursula's Speak Your Way to More Clients class. My jaw dropped.

This is exactly what I need. She doesn't even know that I've started a speaking business and am writing a book. She's told me, "When you put yourself out there and believe in what you're doing, what you need next will show up." She wasn't kidding.

I walked into the class with my list of questions, and Ursula had the answers. I took notes feverishly and left the class completely satisfied. With all of this new information and the upcoming release of my book, I could hardly contain my excitement.

Three months later, Ursula offered 30 minutes of free coaching and personally invited me to join her Quantum Leap Mastermind, which was a $200 per month investment.

Concerned about the money, but sure that working with Ursula was going to help, I said yes. Good thing I did!

During my one-on-one coaching in the first mastermind, Ursula asked what I was charging for my workshops. When I told her, she responded, "It's too low," and shared current industry pricing.

My heart sank into my stomach. *WHAT?*

"I'm not comfortable charging that." The words flew out of my mouth. She spent some time trying to convince me that what I was doing warranted higher pricing, but I couldn't wrap my head around it. "Let me get a few paid speaking jobs under my belt, and then I'll increase my fee."

Not much later, Ursula shared that she was discontinuing the program, as it didn't feel right anymore.

What am I going to do without these meetings? And then I

thought, *It's okay. I'll be saving $200 every month.*

It was in that moment that I realized how confused I was about money. I was holding on to every dollar I had like it was my last, yet I was afraid to charge appropriately for what I'm worth and what the industry warrants.

Seven months passed, and Ursula reached out, "Wanda, I know you were disappointed about the end of Quantum Leap, and I want to invite you into my new program. I really believe this will help you reach your sales goals even faster..." She shared the details, and asked if I was interested.

It sounded great. "How can I *not* participate? The big question is: How much?"

"It's just under $10,000 for the year."

"Yes, sign me up!"

I gave her my information and put the phone down.

How is it that less than a year ago, I was balking at $200 per month, and now the $800 per month expense is okay? My savings is less than it was when I hesitantly committed to $200 per month. Is it possible that my money beliefs are changing — that my fear of money is dissipating? Am I finally getting it?

A short time later, I had lunch with a friend and told her

about my pricing dilemma. She asked how much I was charging, and I braced myself for her reaction: "Wanda, that's RIDICULOUS!" Amidst the noise in the restaurant, I heard nothing but dead silence.

"What do you think I should charge?" Her answer was *exactly* what Ursula told me. A coincidence? I don't think so!

It's time. I called Ursula and told her I was ready, and synchronicity went to work.

After my keynote at a networking event, I was approached by a sales manager, "Wanda, I'd really like to bring you in to train 30 to 35 members of my staff. Give me a call to discuss the details."

We talked a few days later, and I quoted my new fee. Then he told me he would have 160 employees in attendance.

Did I hear that right? 160? My heart nearly jumped out of my chest. "The quote I gave you was based on 30 to 35. I'll have to rework the numbers and get back to you."

On my coaching call with Ursula the next day, we came up with a quote that made sense for everyone involved.

I can't believe it. I'm submitting my first five-figure proposal!

Before we hung up, Ursula reminded me how much earning potential I have, "Wanda, focus on your money-making opportunities."

Oh my goodness! That's it! I haven't been looking at my earning potential. I've been focusing on my declining savings account. Her words immediately released me. *I feel liberated.* Ursula's advice was just what I needed to push through the limits I'd placed on myself.

I've made the money shift. I finally believe 100% in the value of what I do and know that I deserve to be paid well for it. I'm no longer afraid of money. I don't run from it, and I don't cling to it. Three years ago, I took on Ursula's mantra of "money flows to me easily and effortlessly," but since I've made this money shift, I feel and believe the words with every cell in my body. Recently, we added "a lot of" to the beginning of the mantra.

Ahhh…music to my ears.

 **Wanda Allen** is a speaker, a coach, the author of *Follow Up Savvy*, and an expert at helping entrepreneurs, business owners, and sales professionals to strengthen relationships, increase client retention, protect themselves from competition, become more referable, and improve sales performance by implementing an effective follow up system. Prior to launching Follow Up Savvy, Wanda was a business banker for 25 years in San Diego, where she received extensive training in business development, maintaining client relationships, and customer service. Wanda is also a Senior Manager with *SendOutCards*.

To connect with Wanda, visit
www.followupsavvy.com

The Faith Shift

"Faith is taking the first step even when you don't see the whole staircase."

Martin Luther King, Jr.

The day of the bestseller campaign arrived. I had done everything that I could. My team had done everything they could. Amanda and Janise had shown up to help support me throughout the day. I had other team members supporting me around the country. I had clients emailing me excitedly that they were about to purchase their books.

At this point, it was just time to pray that the day went smoothly, and everyone moved forward with their commitments. It was time to let go. It was time to have faith.

I did my best. It wasn't easy.

I was watching one of the categories that Selling with Intention was in (I believe it was textbooks), but it didn't seem to move. I watched that category for a couple of hours and nothing happened. I panicked — what was going wrong? Every fear that I had came up.

And then my husband texted me, "We are number twelve in Sales and Marketing!" What? I'd been watching a category that didn't move at all. (Now, we think the category wasn't even working that day). Tim had been watching another category and Selling with Intention was moving quickly.

The book kept moving, and we hit #1 in several categories including Sales and Marketing, Business, and others. Out of over 2,000,000 books, we hit #176 overall which blew me away.

I could now say, "I am a #1 Bestselling author of the #1 bestselling book, Selling with Intention."

Who was I not to be a bestselling author?

Keep Going

I have a standing joke with one of my dear friends, Amanda. We have full permission to call each other on those days when we want to give up and say, "That's it, I quit." When we feel like we can't take another step, we always say to each other, "Okay, well, what else would we do?" And then we laugh, and go back to whatever it is we were working on.

I was recently being interviewed by Maurice Dimino, the Sicilian Mentor. He asked me, "When did you know that you were on your path and living your purpose?" I kind of laughed and said, "Do I really know? I still ask myself if I am on the right path. I pray every day that God will show me the way." I then shared how I also give myself permission to quit whenever I need to, and then I call Amanda so I can complain for a few minutes before I get back on track.

"I love it!" Maurice said, "A quitting coach! I'm going to get one!" Exactly. So much of my Faith Shift has been about giving myself permission to quit when I need to. Letting go of thinking that things have to be, or look, a certain way or thinking that I have to know exactly what my path should be. Or letting go of the idea that I have to do things perfectly or say things perfectly. Remember, "Done is better than perfect."

I love the question, *"What would you do if you won the lottery?"* If I won the lottery, I would do this. I would write. I would speak. I would help people shift and expand so they could live their greatest life. Maybe I would have more money to give to charities. Maybe it would be easier to travel wherever I wanted to go in the world. But mostly, I would just do what I am already doing.

What would *you* do if you won the lottery? Would you continue on the path that you are on, or is there another path that is calling you? Staying in your comfort zone is easy for now. But regret is one of the hardest things to swallow later on in life. Les Brown said, "If you put yourself in a position where you have to stretch outside your comfort zone, then you are forced to expand your consciousness." And when we stretch and grow, we will never be left wondering, *What if...?*

Once you choose your One Great Goal, sell with intention and synchronicity, and decide to live your dream, will you stick with it long enough? The only way to stick with it is to keep the faith. The only way to keep going through the tough times is to keep the faith. The only way to live outside of your comfort zone — your belief zone — is to keep the faith. Get it?

Keeping the faith is not easy to do when you have run out of money, run out of courage, or have just plain given up. However, that is the exact time when you have to keep it. Remember what Napoleon Hill said — when you're ready to give up, you just might be "three feet from gold."

Do you know how many times I have wanted to give up? How many times *today* I have wanted to give up? I've lost count. Okay, I am being a bit facetious, but if we are honest with ourselves, there are moments when we all want to quit.

Being an entrepreneur or sales professional is tough, especially after living through the last great repression. Was it a recession? A depression? Who cares, because either way, it changed the way you do business, and you either repressed yourself and what you really desired to do, or you did something new in your business and decided to survive and thrive. And, even if you're worn out, exhausted, and don't think you can keep going, remember that you might just be three feet from gold.

> Keeping the faith is not easy to do when you have run out of money, run out of courage, or have just plain given up. However, that is the exact time when you have to keep it. Remember what Napoleon Hill said — when you're ready to give up, you just might be "three feet from gold."

The faith shift is about continuing on your synchronistic journey even when you are in the middle of perceived challenges. Why do I say, "perceived?" Because our perspective on something determines whether or not it is really a challenge. Sometimes a challenge is just rerouting us on our journey and saving us from something worse. Rather than letting challenges stop you, keep the faith and carry on anyway because your sales and other goals are still waiting for you!

YOU Are the Answer

There is nothing more heartbreaking for me than seeing talented entrepreneurs and sales professionals not fulfilling their potential. By that, I mean they aren't working with the right target clients, they are selling enough to just pay the bills and, overall, they are just *existing*. Well, it's not enough to just exist. Now, more than ever, we live in a world that needs strong leaders from every sector to bring prosperity back. We need YOU.

Whenever you have the truth is that one person at a time, choosing to do more than survive, is the only way to bring this country back to prosperity. It's one person at a time deciding to live a new way. One entrepreneur or sales professional deciding to sell more and give more. That's how we get money moving again in the world.

David Cameron Gikandi, author of *A Happy Pocket Full of Money: Infinite Wealth and Abundance in the Here and Now*, says it like this, "So the next time you have inspiration, rejoice in knowing that a group of people, small or large, is actively asking you and waiting for you to fulfill their desires. In other words, you are the answer to their prayers."

You are the answer to someone's prayers. *YOU*, not someone else.

Do you really understand what that means? It means that someone is in pain somewhere. They have a problem, and they need to fix it. They are praying for the answer or maybe just asking the Universe or themselves, "What do I have to do to fix this?" And then, BAM, you meet this person, or you get inspired to follow up. You are the answer — you are the perfect person to solve their problem. But if you aren't listening to inspiration, if you don't hear the call because you're too busy looking at all of the sales you don't have, then someone else will.

> You are the answer — you are the perfect person to solve their problem. But if you aren't listening to inspiration, if you don't hear the call because you're too busy looking at all of the sales you don't have, then someone else will.

Whenever I am speaking from the stage, I feel so blessed to be able to share my heart with the audience. As I look out at the audience, I see them — I mean I really see them — their dreams, their hopes, their losses, and sadness. It's almost like I see a "sea of dreams" floating above their heads, and I can feel their innermost desires.

But I also feel their lack of faith in themselves, and it breaks my heart. If they could only see what others see in them — what others believe about them and who God created them to be.

If they could only see what a huge disservice they are doing to the world, and their potential clients, when they stop themselves from picking up the phone and calling a client. Or, when they stop themselves from closing the sale because they question themselves, their products, etc. When they let their fear stop them from giving someone else the opportunity to choose their product or service, they stop the flow of prosperity. In my worldview, the entire flow stops when each one of us stops.

And when YOU ask for the sale, when you keep the faith, the wheel starts turning again and the money begins flowing. Faith tells us that there is more than enough for everyone. There is prosperity. There is flow. There is hope. There is possibility. There is synchronicity.

Think about it. What if YOU really are the answer to someone's prayers? What if only YOU can make that difference for someone? Will you pick up the phone now?

As I was writing this book, my clients were writing their chapters about the synchronistic shifts they've made since being part of the Synchronize MasterMind. It was really difficult for me to actually read their chapters and receive their gratitude. Yes, they made money shifts, but the shifts they made around faith and self-belief were the ones that brought tears to my eyes. Why? Because I know that once you make a shift in your self-belief, or in your belief about what's possible, no one can ever take that away from you, and it can serve you for the rest of your life.

On the days that I want to quit, I will reach down and pick up a copy of *Selling with Synchronicity* and turn to their chapters, and I will be reminded why I need to keep going.

Sell and Speak from the Heart

Your faith journey includes speaking and selling from the heart. When I speak, I show a picture of a man with a hammer in his hand, pointed at his head. And right next to it, I have a picture of a heart. My message is simple: "Get out of your head and get into your heart. Stop thinking so much with your head and think with your heart." What do I mean by that?

When you are in your head, you are using your left brain to logically figure it out. But what if you can't figure it out? What if you acted from your heart, which is more of a right brain focus? What if you focused more on your heart and changing people's lives? When you sell, speak, and act from your heart, you make it all about the client and not about you. Focusing on the client allows you to get out of the way, so that selling can happen easily and effortlessly. And I promise that the money will follow.

I was speaking at a NAWBO group a few months ago. After I spoke, one of my clients was in the room, and she stood up and shared one of the most heart-felt testimonials I have ever heard. She had just finished writing her first book, was speaking on it frequently, and had just restructured some of her products. I could see where she was going and what was ahead for her. I knew she couldn't see the entire picture yet, but I could see it.

We connected briefly after the event, and I thanked her for her kind words. She looked me in the eye and said, "Yes, and I really meant it. You've made a huge difference in my business and in my life." I received what she was saying even though I felt myself choking up. I don't know about you, but it's hard to receive such powerful gratitude at times. (I'm working on that!)

My client kept popping into my mind, and I kept thinking how much I'd like to work with her again. We had launched our new mastermind programs, and I had a new group opening up, and I kept thinking about her. Then a little voice in my head would say, "Yes, but she probably won't pay for another program." Her face popped up relentlessly, and I finally just emailed her. I explained the new program and asked if she was interested.

To be 100% truthful, I did not think she was going to sign up. Not even a little bit. So when we finally connected, I was completely detached from the outcome. We chatted without expectation, and I talked to her from the heart. I wanted to know what was going on with her. I wanted to know what she was planning on doing next in her business. After she shared, I knew she was a perfect fit. She finally said, "So, are you going to tell me about the mastermind?"

Even after years of selling, my heart still pounds during a sale because my intention is so strong to make it about them, and I want to make sure they know I am coming from that space. I quickly shared the highlights of what would be covered in the group and then I stopped. Silence. I could hear her breathing. And then she said, "I'm so in!"

> Faith tells us to shift out of doubt and to keep following the inspiration, offering the opportunity, asking them if it feels like a good fit.

Faith tells us to shift out of doubt and to keep following the inspiration, offering the opportunity, asking them if it feels like a good fit.

Surrender to Something Big

As a child, my family attended a small Lutheran Church in Minnesota. I had wonderful Sunday school teachers and pastors who really helped me on my journey. St. Paul's Lutheran Church is an ELCA, or Evangelical Lutheran

Church of America. ELCA is what many would say is the most "liberal" denomination of the Lutheran faith. My experiences here laid the foundation for my faith in God's plan for my life. And while I didn't really want to talk about religion in this book, I find it unavoidable as I write this chapter on faith. The point is, I don't care what religion you are. I do hope that you believe in something bigger than you, call it God, call it the Universe, I don't care. When you believe in something bigger than you, you surrender and easily move into the flow of synchronicity and God's plan of prosperity for you.

One of my *Great Goals* has been to become an international speaker so I could impact the prosperity in people's lives around the world. Let me be clear, I did not choose that goal. I felt like that goal chose me because it is one of the reasons I am on this planet. I didn't know when or how that would show up, but I had a deep knowing that this journey on earth wasn't really about me but more about the message I would be teaching.

Before I go up to speak on stage, I always say a prayer, "God, please guide me today. Please allow the right words to come through me for whoever needs to hear them. Amen." That's it. I ask for God's guidance because I know that what He has to say through me is more powerful than anything I could make up.

The more I surrender and get out of the way, the more powerful the ideas that come through and the more great opportunities show up. As humans, we like to be in control, we like to know what's coming next, and we like to be prepared. But that's not always possible. I truly believe that God's plan is so much bigger than we can imagine, and we have to get out of the way for it to unfold. I feel God's hand in everything I do when I surrender.

On the other hand, when I try to do it "my way," I get stuck, and things don't work for me. When I get attached to my outcome, things stop flowing. There will be times when what you want doesn't show up the way you want it to or the way you intended it to. Faith is about detachment. In my experience, when I have held on really tightly to a prospect, trying to "will them" into being my client, it has never worked.

> The more I surrender and get out of the way, the more powerful the ideas that come through and the more great opportunities show up.

When I have let go, and come from my heart, knowing that I can really help, they almost always sign up.

I have proof of prayers answered and redirected journeys, so I believe in God, and I am not afraid of what's ahead. I am only afraid of not serving enough people before I leave this planet. People will judge me for these beliefs. And people will judge you. Stay strong in who you are and what you believe about faith and your journey because those beliefs are sacred.

Divine Downloads and Intervention

As I've already shared, there have been moments when my husband and I have faced losing everything, and I mean *everything*. A few years ago, our real estate losses had piled up, we owed investors thousands of dollars, and there were countless other challenges. The good and bad news was that we made too much money to file for Chapter 7 bankruptcy, which would have eliminated all of our debt. It is a choice that many people make, and I don't judge that choice for others. We just knew it wasn't the best choice for us. Our desire was to pay every single investor back, even when others said it was a bad idea since they had taken on the risk as well. We didn't care. We wanted to do what we thought was right.

I distinctly remember a day when I felt completely broke and broken. The weight of the money we owed was on my shoulders, and I was no longer sure that I could sell my way out of the debt. Together, Tim and I were making a lot of money, but with our past investment mistakes, it just wasn't enough. There were months when we paid six mortgages at the same time, without renters in the properties. On that particular day, I remember completely breaking down, hitting the floor on my knees and just praying. I asked God, "What should we do?" and I heard, "Be patient. Pay it off, one bill at a time." Patience wasn't my strength, and I knew it was time that I worked on that.

The words that came through that day were Divine Downloads. Although it seemed obvious, I knew it was exactly what we needed to do. We needed a plan to pay every penny back and to restore our financial balance. Tim and I came together and created the plan. Once it was down on paper, it looked much easier than I thought, although we were still over $100,000 in past expenditures (Thank you Access Consciousness!). Somewhere in me, I knew we could do it. I knew we could get out.

When you get committed and ask for help, help shows up. Angels showed up on my journey to help us figure out the best and fastest way to pay all of our past expenditures back. Others advised us to break it into bite-sized chunks. My mastermind members from  Loral Langemeier's Big Table program listened to my challenges and reminded me that not only was it possible

> When you get committed and ask for help, help shows up.

to get it all paid back, but there was a way to do it much faster than I had imagined. The more I shared with people, the more people shared their own challenges with me. Obviously, we weren't the only ones going through difficult financial times. (Duh!) People shared that they had lost businesses, homes, life savings, and more. Looking back, I am so grateful that I shared our tough stuff because it gave other people the permission to share theirs out loud and figure it out as well.

Breakdowns usually lead to breakthroughs. Sometimes we need to hit the floor on our knees to find our way back up. I can assure you, though, that you are never alone. And remember, our breakthroughs are usually as large as our breakdowns.

Speaking of breakdowns, I have one more shift to share, but it's one that usually happens in between all of these shifts and sometimes during them.

I call it the In-between...

Keeping the Faith in Love & Business

by Susan Sheppard

So what is happening? Why can't I move forward? This year is almost gone, and I haven't landed one new client. I love what I do, but this can't continue.

I know I make a difference in the world. It's never been a doubt for me. Synchronicity has been part of my life for at least thirty years, and I adopted a "there are no accidents" philosophy in that part of my learning curve that has served me in every facet of my life and really reduced the pain. Yet, in the process of rebirthing my latest business, Getting What You Want (Life and Relationship Coaching), my faith has been sorely tested.

In the five minutes between opening my eyes and dragging myself out of bed, I had moved from anxiety to palpable panic. I headed to the kitchen.

Come on, Susan. You can figure this out. I gave myself my best effort at a pep talk as I poured my coffee and sat down, but the doubt was too loud.

How can I deal with this mountain of debt? How can I help the kids move on and out of my house? How can I continue doing what I love?

I finished my cup of coffee, without even a glimmer of enlightenment.

I have achieved every goal I have ever seriously attempted because of my one great goal that revealed itself at the first Synchronize MasterMind: Meditate daily, do what is in front of me, and stay in the flow. Why should this one be different?

Morning meditation done, and still nothing.

I headed to my J.O.B., where at this rate, I would still be working when I was ninety years old, and I confirmed a few strategy sessions. Taking the next step in front of me felt good, as I chose faith over doubt.

Something good is going to happen today. Great things have already begun happening in my life...

For a moment, I took inventory and was reminded of the moment my faith in the Universe and my ability to see and enjoy synchronicity had been incinerated...literally.

Seven years prior, I had driven home from a long day of Christmas shopping to find my home engulfed in flames. Life as I knew it ended that day, and somehow, the magic had gone. It took three years and a lawsuit, and I found myself with a new home, and a mountain of debt. I was doing what I love (helping people with broken hearts to heal and find loving relationships), yet I still had to keep this J.O.B. to pay the bills. And when the Real Estate market crashed, my kids were forced to remain in my home.

In the midst of this chaos, I encountered this amazing, brilliant, spiritual young woman who reminded me that I lived and loved synchronicity for thirty years before the fire. I met Ursula at a business-building event, and I was touched by her confidence and concern for others. I saw the magic in her.

At her Sales Coach Now-LIVE event, I tuned out the mind chatter. *You are running out of funds and time, Susan. Something has to shift soon.* I chose to believe Ursula and stay open to possibility.

Get Loved Now. The words floated through my head. *I will have my own event!* The excitement coursed through me, until the doubt crept in.

Susan, you don't have the money. How will you fill the room? What are you thinking?

Interrupting the chatter, I checked the domain Get Loved Now on my phone. The .com was available, and I bought it. Then the vision enlarged: A beautiful white and crystal room, filled with guests, and a series of speakers, all focused on helping women get ready for and attract love into their lives.

We could work together to help the single, lonely, wounded, wronged, cheated-on women, and I could launch my Get Loved Now membership there.

I knew this was a "Yes."

Synchronicity kicked in, and the Universe delivered a perfect combination of brilliant speakers who were not only excited but available for the date I had picked. In hardly any time at all, I had my team ready to support women on topics ranging from abuse, to transition, to money, to spirituality, to fitness, to image, and of course, to relationships.

The only problem was the location. My team had been unable to find an available location in the entire Los Angeles area. Less than two months before the event, I was stressing about it when traffic forced me off the 101 freeway and onto Ventura Blvd, where I noticed the Sportsmen's Lodge.

Well, it's dark and masculine, but it would be better than a tent!

I pulled in and walked toward the event center. I could not believe my eyes. It not only looked exactly like the white and crystal room I had envisioned, it was available.

It's magic — synchronicity! The excitement was reminiscent of life before the fire.

The day arrived, and everything flowed. The event was perfect…except it wasn't profitable. No new clients, and I still had to pay for the event.

It was two weeks later that I woke up in a panic, knowing that the log jam had to clear soon, or I was going to be in serious trouble.

I choose faith. The Universe will deliver. I just need to stay in action and do what is in front of me.

By 4p.m., nothing had changed.

I set my intention for the last strategy session of the day and picked up the phone.

After a quick greeting, she interrupted, "Susan, I am a really smart, successful woman. I just don't know how to 'do' relationships. I have read your book several times, and I need help."

"Then let's get to work…" I asked her questions to clarify where she was and where she wanted to be, and then I took a deep breath before asking: "Do you know what to do next? Would you like some help?"

"Yes, where do I sign up?"

Catching my breath, I shared the investment for the year-long program, and she enrolled immediately. After we hung up, I processed the payment and thanked the Universe for delivering.

The phone rang again, and my daughter's excited voice caught me by surprise, "Mom, we were approved to rent the house and are signing lease papers right now!"

"Honey, that is wonderful!"

Wow, a new client, and my house back — all in the same day?

She finished telling me about the house, and we hung up.

The phone rang again. This time, it was Liz, my unpaid assistant who was relying on her real estate business to provide while I got my stuff together. "Susan, I don't know what's going on today, but I have leased two houses. It's so strange! Nothing has happened on these for months, and all of a sudden, I have clients everywhere!"

Wow! What an amazing day!

I climbed into bed that night, feeling relieved, excited, and amazed.

Did all of this really just happen?

And then the phone rang again.

My heart began to race as I looked at the screen. It was the man I had fallen in love with last year — the one who had disappeared without explanation.

"Susan, I have to apologize for the way I left you last year. What we had was so good. I just needed to call and tell you that I am sorry it didn't work out..." He told me what had driven his decision, and his sincerity washed over me.

"I was never angry with you. On some level, I knew that was the reason..." We talked for hours and ended the conversation as loving friends.

I laid my head on that pillow, grateful that I had kept the faith. My heart was full. Synchronicity? Yes!

In one day, the flow of wealth surged, my intuition is validated, my home is my own again, and the possibility of love has opened up and descended upon me. Thank you, Universe! Thank you, Ursula!

And then, two weeks later, I was made aware that a relative whom I had loved dearly had passed away unexpectedly and left me a portion of his substantial estate.

Now, I really can retire from my J.O.B. and build a legacy with my message of passion, sacred intimacy, and love.

The Universe works in mysterious ways, and I am so grateful to Ursula for helping me to remember that I can have faith in, and live in the magic of, synchronicity again.

Susan Sheppard is the founder of Getting What You Want, a life and relationship coaching organization created to help women get exactly what they want in every facet of their life. She is the author of the book *How to Get What You Want From Your Man Anytime*, a relationship book that shows everyone in romantic relationships how to be content and have more fun, more sex, and less bickering. Susan is a speaker, writer, trainer, and coach who is passionate about sacred intimacy and on a crusade to end indifferent relationships. With an intense, straight-talking, compassionate manner, she targets the core issues and quickly moves you in the direction of getting what you want. She enrolls you in her passionate movement towards meaningful love and life.

To connect with Susan, visit her at
www.gettingwhatyouwant.com

The In-Between Shift

"At fifteen life had taught me undeniably that surrender, in its place, was as honorable as resistance, especially if one had no choice."

Maya Angelou

In September of 2011, I went to Tahoe for the second time to meet with my mastermind group at Loral's Big Table. The weeks leading up to Tahoe were really stressful because I kept questioning everything regarding the Amazon Bestseller campaign.

"Will the campaign really work, or will I fail?"

"Will I sell enough books or fall short?"

Panic came up. And then I surrendered, "Forget it! I cannot think about this anymore! I am just going to surrender, enjoy Tahoe, and have faith that it will all work out!"

So I let go, and I went to Tahoe. Loral happened to be in the middle of her own New York Times bestseller campaign and I remember asking the room a lot of questions, just to make sure my bases were covered. Loral asked me some questions about my campaign, and I answered them. And the general consensus in the room was that my plan wasn't going to work.

And then one of the trainers spoke up from the back of the room, "She'll hit it. Her plan will work. I've seen a lot of them, and with the numbers she's talking about, she'll hit it."

It was the exact God Nod I needed in that moment, in the In-between, to keep going. It reminded me that when I let go and get out of the way, synchronicity steps in.

Those six months between the day I announced my bestseller campaign and the day Selling with Intention became a bestseller represented the In-between, or that time between the creation of the idea and the actualization of the idea. They were a long six months — or at least it seemed that way to me. There were many times when I wanted to give up or hide. I mean, I had made a public announcement that Selling with Intention was going to be a bestselling book! Was I crazy?

The In-between gave me the space to dream, create, and know that by answering the question, "What is the fastest and easiest way to get there?" I would create the plan that would give me the greatest flow and synchronicity. And it did.

I never underestimate the power of the In-between. In fact, I now treasure those spaces.

The Space Between

After moving from the Inland Empire back to Orange County (for those who don't know, that's only about thirty miles in California), I became really clear that I was in a new, unexplored space. I call it a "space" because it felt like I was in-between one thing and something else. I was leaving the past behind and stepping into a new future. Yet, there was this distinguishable feeling, this space, that I could very clearly sense. Because I didn't understand the space, I called it the In-between.

Over the next couple of weeks, I was busy traveling around the country to speak and participate in retreats, and I began to share this feeling of the In-between. I should not have been surprised to find people using those two words together quite effortlessly, as if they had been saying them forever. As I peered deeper, with wonder, into the In-between, it started to shift from a frightening place of change and unpredictability, to a safe spot that I might like to stay in for a while. Or, at least visit more.

> The In-between is that space in the middle of before and after. It is that space of non-creation.

The In-between is that space in the middle of before and after. It is that space of non-creation. I was speaking to an artist, Lise, about the "space," and she said, "Yes, of course, the In-between." Curious, I asked her what she meant since the words had so effortlessly fallen from her tongue. She explained that as an artist, she often finds herself in the In-between, when she is finished with one artistic project and beginning to dream about, but not yet commit to, the new project. The blank canvas.

Yes! This was the space I had been in since I left the Inland Empire. I knew I was in a time of transition and creation, but I didn't want to put a name on it or define it in any way. I wanted to revel in this space of not knowing what was coming next. A space of zero expectations. A space of, well, space.

The Shift Inside the Shift

I believe this space — this In-between — occurs before, during, and after all of the shifts I have shared throughout this book. In fact, I believe it happens whenever you say *yes* to expanding your sales, your business, or your life in some way. It happens when you finish a project or reach a goal, and then you ask, "Now what?"

You say *yes* to possibility, and then you find yourself outside of your comfort zone — in that space where you have a choice: 1) you can get scared because you have no idea what you just said yes to, or how it's going to happen, or 2) you can relax into it and wait, be still, and listen.

Most people, when they don't know what's happening, get into that space and suddenly feel scared, anxious, or even angry or depressed. It's that moment when all of your old fears and limiting beliefs will invite you back to a place where you can think and play small again, because it's "comfortable" because it's known. It's that moment when something triggers the voice that tells you that "you can't" or "it's not worth the work."

Sometimes, you see it coming; and sometimes, it catches you by surprise. Sometimes, it starts with a case of the "Forget-it's," or that other F-word we sometimes use when the pressure becomes too great.

The truth is that on this journey, there will be days when you want to quit. These moments are when the In-between is not a luxurious stopping point; rather it becomes a necessity because you've had a bad day. A bad month. A bad year. It's when that last straw falls on the camel's back. The day I planned to write this chapter was one of those days.

I'd had a wonderful night's sleep, and I woke up feeling like it was Christmas. I had an exciting day planned of fun meetings, working on my book, and driving down by the ocean. That was it. It was destined to be a fantastic day, and I couldn't wait to get started!

But I made the mistake of picking up my phone and looking at my texts and email before I headed out the door, and there were two messages that completely set me off. I won't go into detail to protect the innocent, but let's just say they made me really angry because someone had accused me of something that simply wasn't true. It was their "stuff" coming up, and I knew that they knew it wasn't true. They just wanted to be a jerk, and it wasn't the first time. I was over it, and it induced a serious case of the Forget-its.

> The Forget-its give me perspective. And magic *does* happen.

"That's it! I am quitting everything!" Throwing myself fully into the tantrum, I stomped down the stairs, got into my car, and drove to the ocean. I decided to go with it and surrender to it.

Throughout the day, the emails and text bothered me, but I just kept saying, "Forget it! Who cares?"

While it sounds negative, having a case of the Forget-its is more valuable than you might imagine. When you know what's happening, and you totally surrender, you let go of everything that is, everything you've wanted, and you just say, "I don't care. Forget it," you make room for magical things to happen.

Throughout my career, I have had many cases of the Forget-its, and I have learned to thoroughly enjoy every single one of them. You might be surprised that I say "enjoy" them, but I do. I swim around in them for an entire day. They make me smile and laugh again. They make me turn the music up really loud in my car and open up my windows. They make me realize that in the bigger scheme of things, what I am upset about really doesn't matter. The Forget-its give me perspective.

And magic *does* happen. In the middle of my tantrum, on the day I was to write this chapter, in the middle of the Forget-its, I had three powerful *paid* speaking engagements show up. I cannot explain this phenomenon. All I can tell you is that, in my experience, stepping into the Forget-its can deliver powerful results and allow you to shift back into synchronicity.

So, the next time you are having a bad day, I hope that you, too, will enjoy your case of the Forget-its — or that other F-word we sometimes use.

What If...?

I would be lying if I said that there aren't times when I am terrified. There are definitely moments of great fear. But over time, I've learned how to quickly replace those moments with faith, knowing that sometimes the best thing to do is to be still. I've learned to create the space between the moments before I allow the paintbrush to "touch the canvas" — to enjoy that delicious, yummy space.

It took a while, but the In-between has started to feel normal. Well, a new normal. Once I realized that the In-between was more than just my experience of transition — that it was a space that could be created at any time by simply summoning it and taking a moment to experience it — magical things began to happen.

I began to wonder: What would happen if I created the In-between whenever I was stuck, or whenever I felt like I was forcing something, like a sale? What would happen?

Perhaps the In-between wasn't such a big secret after all? It seemed like everyone I talked to had experienced it in some way. But the question remained, had they used it as a tool? As a noun? A place to visit? For example, "Wait, don't talk to me right now, I'm in the In-between?"

Joseph Campbell said, "We must be willing to let go of the life we have planned, so as to accept the life that is waiting for us." The only way to do this is to step into the

In-between. The life you've been living, the business or career you've created, does not have to define you. It's not your final stop. Give yourself permission to paint on a new canvas.

> The life you've been living, the business or career you've created, does not have to define you. It's not your final stop.

Creating the In-between

Sometimes we just need a little space. Or, a lot of space. And we need to create it for ourselves. In *Selling with Intention*, I shared the idea of creating an "Intentional Schedule" to help you design a life that supports you and your sales goals. In addition to having time to sell and run your business, it is also just as important (if not more so) to create time in your schedule to just be. Or to create. Or to have fun. Or to do whatever it is that you *know* you need to do that day.

There have been times when I have created the In-between because I needed a break to simply be. Other times, the In-between has been created to spend time enjoying life — going out with friends, getting a massage, or jogging along the seashore. Do whatever recharges you and puts the spark back into your life. The point is, you can create this space anytime and anywhere that you need to. It might be for a very short amount of time (on a flight from Los Angeles to Minneapolis), or it might be for a longer period of time (a month or even a year). When I look back on my life, there have been many times when I have spent time in this space.

Another great example of the In-between was the three-month summer break I used to have in grade school and high school. I always looked forward to that time because it allowed me to experience new things and have new adventures. It was a welcome change in the routine. Perhaps we are conditioned to crave or create that delicious space so we can reinvent ourselves — and our lives.

When we don't create our own In-between space, then it is sometimes created for us. I have seen illness take people quickly to that space to give them time to re-evaluate how they have been spending their life and their time.

Our deepest desires and goals will always try to surface, even when we try to push them down. What you really want also wants you, and you have to choose it. Creating In-between space can give you the time you need to consider all of your options and make a choice that really serves you. Remember, though, the In-between is a place to visit, not a place to live. If the In-between becomes a place you stay too long, it could lead to depression, anxiety, or other unwelcome feelings — stagnation of all that you really want to create.

As I write this, I am 30,000 feet in the air on a Southwest flight en route from Los Angeles to Minneapolis.

Whenever I fly, I rediscover this incredible In-between space to get work done, write, journal, read, or just daydream. What's really interesting is that on any given flight, I can complete a couple days of work in just a few hours because there aren't any distractions. Which reminds me, I've decided to travel more!

What is your In-between? What could creating that space in your life do for you?

Surrendering to the Chaos

by Tanya Brown

Chaos has always been a part of my life. If I wasn't thrown into the middle of it, I found or created it myself. Almost two decades after the shocking death of my sister Nicole Brown Simpson, my family and I are still living in perpetual chaos. And it's not just the media craze anymore. By 2009, we were dealing with Mom's stage 3C breast cancer and Dad's dementia shifting into full-blown Alzheimers. I decided to move home, thinking I could help, finish graduate school, and start my business.

What? I know. What was I thinking?

But I love helping other people, and I knew that with my life experience — suffering challenges with self-identity, eight deaths during my high school years and numerous other losses, an eating disorder, and suicidal ideations — I could meet hurting people where they are and lead them out of the darkness I knew so well. And maybe, if I caught them early enough, I could help them avoid some of the pain.

Two years after moving home and working through school, the desire to help others became intense, and graduate school didn't feel like the answer anymore. *I have to find a way to do this for a living, so I can do it full-time and support my family.*

It wasn't long before synchronicity gave me the invitation — through a friend — to begin learning how to make money doing what I love. I found myself with a paid ticket to Loral Langemeier's 3 Days to Cash and a synchronistic meeting with a sales coach that would change my life.

It didn't take long in that room for me to realize that if I didn't speak up and share who I am, who I intend to serve, and why, then I can never grow a business. So, the first thing I had to do was own the fact that I am Nicole's sister, and that the experience of walking the journey I did is part of what qualifies me to help others walk through the type of pain I was in. It was a big step.

The next thing I had to face was my negative perception of sales people. If I was going to sell, I couldn't keep believing that to be successful, I would have to be pushy, salesy, and unconcerned with the good of humanity. That's how I had felt about *all* sales people. Was I wrong! When I saw people around me, in service and helping others, I realized how wrong I had been, and the shifting continued.

And then Loral asked me to develop a sales system *(What's that?)* with the help of a group of ten people and a coach in the room. I was drawn to the group with the beautiful and obviously confident Ursula Mentjes, yet I struggled through the group activity, realizing how much I didn't want to talk about my offerings. But I knew that if I didn't tell people, I would be doing them a disservice. I was finally learning that selling could be serving.

Slowly, I was shifting. The idea of serving others, while creating a sound financial future, was beginning to feel more comfortable.

Where did I start to believe that service and abundance do not belong together?

And then I thought of my family. For years, we were ridiculed and scrutinized for making money off of Nicole's death.

What they did not see was the incredible outreach we were doing *because* of the story. This mentality had stuck with me. *I have been afraid to market my services for fear of being ridiculed and scrutinized. And I have been terrified of success, not failure.*

The shift happened in the room with Loral and Ursula. I felt something profound changing in my soul. I was feeling motivated and ambitious, and finally seeing that I can have what they have too. At the end of the workshop, I asked Ursula for help with the funnel and spreadsheets. She graciously coached me and offered to be there if I ever got stuck again.

A few months later, I sat in Ursula's Sales Coach Now-LIVE event, surrounded by people with the same passion, focus, and ambition to help others. She invited me to a special VIP breakfast to share the Synchronize MasterMind opportunity. I felt my heart race and my palms begin to sweat. *I can't afford this program, but I have to do it.* I signed up, and then the life chaos dial got turned up.

I found out that a friend had relapsed into alcoholism, and that a client at the rehab center where I worked had committed suicide. My dad's mental health began to decline rapidly, my house became even more chaotic, and no one seemed to see or understand my overwhelm. *How am I going to finish school and get this business going in this chaos?* It seemed that every time I engaged in professional responsibilities, there would be an interruption. Someone needed something, and my space was constantly invaded. Between the coursework, counseling individuals and groups, monitoring supervisions, and helping more with my family, I was finding it hard to enjoy the life I was working to create, let alone work on my business.

And the results of the stress were evident. I hurt my arm dealing with fighting dogs, and even got bit by one as I scurried past him while he was chewing on a bone. I misplaced important items constantly. No matter what I did, I could not keep order in my home, head, or life. I began to lose patience. When I started to feel extremely impatient and frustrated about life, I realized I couldn't do it anymore. I couldn't keep trying to keep it all together. I felt so much pressure, and I had to let go of some of it.

"Ursula, I wish I could drop out of this group." It was the third coaching call, and I was tired of not getting all of the work done. "I wish I could sign up next year because there is too much going on with the demands of graduate school, practicum work, and the business. I don't get the projections sheet, and I'm just discouraged. I should be further along by now."

"Tanya, I can't imagine the stress of helping to caregive, getting a degree, and trying to start a business. You *are* dealing with a lot. But please don't give up on this. This won't last forever. You are in the In-between, and your day will come. You can do this."

"I know you're right. Somehow, I know I'm supposed to be here. But what can I get done in the midst of this chaos? Forget it! I'm just going to do what I can do."

And then, somehow, in the midst of the chaos, things started to happen. The first thing I wanted to do was rework my website. *But where will I get the money?* Almost as soon as I asked the question, my boyfriend offered to fund it. *Who will help me?* Again, Ursula referred me to an amazing graphic designer and copywriter. It took hardly any time at all to make this happen.

I finally began to feel like I was not alone on this journey… and that it was okay to ask for help. Many times I felt alone with my challenges, but I was not. Ursula was there. Her team was supporting me. Her referrals had the skills to make it all happen.

And then the magic really started to happen! I plan on writing a book on my life journey in order to help others on similar journeys, so I reached out to Ursula's book coach Amanda. Knowing there would be plenty of legal hoops to jump through because of the story with Nicole, she connected me with her attorney who then introduced me to an entertainment attorney who can help me when I'm ready.

Asking people for what I needed gave me the courage to step outside of my comfort zone and ask one of my friends — another Tanya! — to help me launch my services. She was out of work, and I thought it would help both of us to work together. She said yes, and we started brainstorming ways to get our message out there and help women in pain.

"Tanya, have you heard of the Midwest Center? They sell products on infomercials to help people reduce stress and anxiety. What if there's some way to work with them?"

"Let's call to see if they need someone to help them promote their product."

They not only said yes — they put me on their home page and gave me my own landing page. Now, I have an affiliate link on my site that will give them more exposure and make me some money. *I didn't need to stress myself out to create my own product in the midst of this chaos! Hey, I wonder if...?*

"Do you think they would want to provide workshops and coaching for people who have gone through their program and maybe even for those who haven't?"

"No harm in asking."

They said YES! So, we are in the process of launching live workshops, webinars, and coaching via Midwest Center's product.

This journey has taught me a lot about myself and synchronicity. In the beginning, I wondered how I could do any of this with the chaos around me. But now, I wonder if it was the chaos forcing the surrender that pushed me and all my limiting beliefs out of the way so synchronicity could begin to happen.

Ten years after the murder of her sister, Nicole Brown Simpson, **Tanya Brown** suffered a mental breakdown. After healing her own life with the help of in-patient and out-patient programs, Tanya determined to help others facing extreme loss and pain. Working on her graduate degree, Tanya is blending her professional education with her personal experiences to help others develop effective coping skills to manage stress, anxiety, and depression — to acknowledge their despair and overwhelm, take extremely good care of themselves, and acquire the strategies they need to turn their obstacles into opportunities. As a certified life coach, Tanya helps others help themselves by providing tools for heightened mental clarity and awareness and empowering them to remain disciplined and focused so they will reach their ultimate goal of optimum mental wellness.

To connect with Tanya, visit
www.tanyabrown.net

Living the 7 Shifts

"Until one is committed, there is hesitancy, the chance to draw back. Concerning all acts of initiative (and creation), there is one elementary truth, the ignorance of which kills countless ideas and splendid plans: that the moment one definitely commits oneself, then Providence moves too. All sorts of things occur to help one that would never otherwise have occurred. A whole stream of events issues from the decision, raising in one's favor all manner of unforeseen incidents and meetings and material assistance, which no man could have dreamed would have come his way. Whatever you can do, or dream you can do, begin it. Boldness has genius, power, and magic in it. Begin it now."

William H Murray

Having Selling with Intention hit #1 on Amazon was just the beginning.

What I didn't realize was that I had not only shattered my own beliefs regarding how difficult it could be to create a bestseller campaign — I had shattered the beliefs of everyone in my core community.

Many people asked me how I did it, and when I told them it was "easy" and directed them to my Amazon Bestseller page to see how I had accomplished it, they believed me. Once they believed it themselves, they created simple Amazon bestseller campaigns that didn't cost them a lot of money either.

And, what was even more amazing is that they were reaching bestseller status by selling hundreds of books, not thousands.

The bestseller campaign reminded us all that selling with synchronicity really can be fun AND easy.

7 Shifts in Motion

At the end of 2011, after a very successful, and sometimes stressful year lived outside of my belief and comfort zone, I decided to let it all go. It was as if many of my classes and programs had finished their cycle and something new was being born, but I wasn't sure what it was. So I stepped into the In-between to let the ideas come through. The In-between gave me the space to create even more powerful programs for my clients that would help them get to the next level in their sales.

When I look back, I recognize that I saw the 7 Inner Shifts in motion, and I want to share what transpired so you can see that sometimes the shifts happen very quickly and sometimes they unfold slowly over a year or more. There is no *right* or *wrong* way for them to unfold; there is only *your* way.

> "Oh my goodness…look at what I just did! It's great but… why doesn't all of this other stuff feel right anymore? I don't want to continue with my current classes and programming. What's possible now?"

Yes, when you are crystal clear on your goals, and you allow synchronicity to step in, the shifts can happen faster than you might imagine. Plus, when you are willing to do the work on yourself and let go of those things that are no longer working, the shifts pick up speed.

I know this, because in a matter of a few months, I moved through the 7 Inner Shifts — letting go of most of my classes and programs, creating brand new ones, and quadrupling my prices. It can happen fast!

The Next Quantum Shift

After the dust settled with the bestseller campaign, I took a break and looked around and said, "Oh my goodness...look at what I just did! It's great but...why doesn't all of this other stuff feel right anymore? I don't want to continue with my current classes and programming. What's possible now?"

Breaking through the paradigm of the Amazon Bestseller campaign showed me so clearly how powerful the Quantum Shift had been in that journey. Seeing the evidence reminded me that anything was possible. I just needed to get clear on what I wanted so that synchronicity could kick in!

The Clarity Shift

At the end of 2011, I was up in Tahoe again with my own mastermind members at Loral's *Big Table*. Working with my coach and mastermind group, I got the clarity I needed and designed a new virtual class. Instead of having in-person classes on Selling with Intention and One Great Goal, we revamped my programs to include a virtual course that would fast-track my clients through the sales process virtually. Instead of Quantum Leap, I created a powerful, year-long Synchronize MasterMind that includes in-person sessions with the group, personal coaching with me, and lots of virtual support in between.

I more than quadrupled my prices for coaching, and our mastermind and my new sales funnel supported the overall business goals that I was holding.

All of that happened over a few days in the glorious space of the In-between.

The momentum created by those new programs carried me quickly into 2012.

The Self-Belief Shift

Hitting #1 on Amazon gave me a new confidence that I didn't have before, but thinking about significantly increasing my prices and changing my business model so dramatically brought up some old limiting beliefs and fears.

I was at the spa with Amanda one day, working on the new sales forms, when the chatter got to be too loud. "Amanda, will you look at this?" I showed her one of the sales forms with the new numbers. "Am I crazy? I'm just wiping out everything I've had going for five years and quadrupling my prices. Will anyone will buy this?"

She looked back at me, shaking her head, "It's about time! You could have been charging this last year!"

Ah, the things we cannot see ourselves! Thank you, Amanda!

The Bold Inspired Action Shift

R elaxing at the spa that day (Yes, the spa is a great space to create the In-between!), I finally got all in. I realized that I had been delivering incredible results over the years, and it was time to say "yes" to the new programs and raising my prices.

> I had also just found out that my step-dad had been diagnosed with cancer, and I knew that creating these new programs would also give me more flexibility when and if I needed to head back to Minnesota on short notice.

On a personal level, I had also just found out that my step-dad had been diagnosed with cancer, and I knew that creating these new programs would also give me more flexibility when and if I needed to head back to Minnesota on short notice. I wanted to be there if my step-dad or mom needed me.

So I took bold inspired action. I made the decision and started telling my core community about the new programs. Specifically, I had to let several Quantum Leap groups know that I was going to be discontinuing their program and launching a new one at Sales Coach Now-LIVE. I explained that this program didn't serve them the way I wanted it to serve them, and that I also needed to create more flexibility in my life.

Not only did they understand, they wanted to be the first to learn about the new programs I was creating. I promised them that they would be the first to know.

Even though I had been afraid of disappointing my clients, they were all actually very excited for me, and it was a reminder that when we stand in our power, we give others permission to do the same.

The Core Community Shift

On February 17, 2012, I launched my third annual Sales Coach Now-LIVE event. We had almost five hundred people registered. But due to the ten tickets each person received when they bought ten copies of *Selling with Intention*, we knew we'd have a high no-show rate because people had been given tickets. (People always need to "put some skin in.") Over the two days, we had almost three hundred attendees — our highest attendance yet! The core community was growing!

I made the announcement of the new Synchronize MasterMind group at a private breakfast the second day of Sales Coach Now-LIVE 2012. I invited the former Quantum Leap members along with others from my core community who I thought would be a great fit for the program, and there were some new faces that showed up, ready to play at the highest level. How exciting!

My hope was that those who committed to the program would be taken on a synchronistic journey that would change their lives and their businesses forever.

The Money Shift

Loral Langemeier and Tom Antion shared the stage with me at Sales Coach Now-LIVE 2012 along with my clients and a panel of experts. I taught the 7 Inner Shifts for the first time, and I was excited to see light bulbs going on, and the feedback was powerful. There were even attendees who would shout things like, "Yes!" as I shared the shifts. The message was being received well, and the energy was palpable in the room. I could see that people were moved.

Attendees were making powerful connections with each other that I heard later led to new joint ventures and partnerships. Attendees also found new clients and created powerful new plans for their businesses. Fear and stressful economy stories streamed over our televisions and online, but during those two days, you would have guessed that we were in boom times!

It was by far our most successful event at *Sales Coach Now*. Even more importantly, we had actualized great financial success as well. That day, we sold well into the six figures, and my belief in what I was doing and the power of synchronicity was confirmed.

The Faith Shift

A t the end of that day, I went out to dinner with Tim, my brother, his wife, and some other friends. We toasted each other and really celebrated the incredible day and the lives that had been changed. I was clear that those who had invested in my programs, Loral's or Tom's, would be moving in the direction of their greatest business dreams and improving their lives. I knew that my mission was being accomplished: entrepreneurs and sales professionals were going to sell more, give back to the organizations they care about, and live a great life. More importantly, I knew that faith had led me there because I had remained focused on my vision.

As we toasted each other, I smiled with gratitude and I thanked God for that moment.

I thanked God for showing me that we live in a *Quantum* world and helping me realize that if I feel like it's time to release all of my old classes and create new ones, I can do it in record time.

I thanked God for giving me the gift of *Clarity*, so that I could figure out what I really wanted to create next.

I thanked God for giving me the tools to release *Self-Limiting Beliefs* and fears so I could live in my Soul Purpose.

I thanked God for helping me take the *Bold Inspired Action* that allowed me to exercise my decision-making muscle so I could teach others to do the same.

I thanked God for giving me wonderful people in my *Core Community* who would reflect back to me that I wasn't crazy, that I shouldn't quit, and that they would be there to catch me if I fell.

I thanked God for allowing me to develop a new relationship with *Money* — one that allows me to give back to the organizations I care about, live a great life, and impact the world in my own unique way.

And finally, I thanked God for sticking with me on this *Faith* journey. Faith reminds me that goals actualize when I take a leap that is much bigger than me, a leap that is outside of my belief zone. It allows me to believe in something that I cannot yet see: "Now faith is the substance of things hoped for, the evidence of things not seen." (Hebrews 11:1 — KJV)

"Now faith is the substance of things hoped for, the evidence of things not seen."

About Ursula Mentjes

Ursula Mentjes is a Best-Selling Author, Sales Expert, Certified Sales Coach, and motivational speaker who specializes in Neuro-Linguistic Programming (NLP) to help her clients reach their highest potential in their careers and businesses. Specifically, she has helped businesses double and triple their sales revenue in as short as two months. Ursula is the best-selling author of *Selling with Intention* and *One Great Goal*. Sales guru Brian Tracy endorsed *Selling with Intention: "This powerful, practical book shows you how to connect with customers by fully understanding the sales process from the inside out. It really works!"*

Ursula honed her skills at an International Technical Training company, starting her career in sales in 1996 and advancing to the position of President in 2001. She was responsible for increasing sales by 90% in one year when she was just 27 years old and the company's annual revenue was in the tens of millions. Ursula attributes her success to setting stretch goals and empowering her employees to be the best that they could be. She is passionate about helping individuals and businesses reach their full potential, so in May of 2004, she founded her own Professional Coaching and Consulting firm that specializes in working with entrepreneurs and sales professionals.

Ursula also holds a Bachelor of Arts Degree in Psychology and Communication from St. Olaf College and a Master of Science Degree in Psychology from California Baptist University. She is a Certified NLP Coach through the NLP Institute of California and a 2006 Graduate of Leadership California. Ursula is also President of the National Association of Women Business Owners of California, Past President of the National Association of Women Business Owners Inland Empire Chapter, Past President of the National Association of Women Business Owners of California, President and a founding member of the Business Resource Connection, on the Advisory Council for the Institute for Women Entrepreneurs, and an Inspire Life Skills Board member. She is also a 2007 and 2011 Spirit of the Entrepreneur Finalist, named one of 951 Magazine's *51 to Watch* in 2008, featured on the talk show Exclusive TV, and the recipient of the 2009 NAWBO-IE A.N.I.T.A. Award. She has shared the stage with bestselling author Loral Langemeier, Tom Antion, Giuliana Rancic, and many others!

A Special Invitation from Ursula

FREE 30-Day Membership on My Sales Coach Now!

Imagine that selling could be fun, easy AND exciting…

If you are ready to **get started with ongoing training and support** on the 7 *Inner Shifts and the Principles of Selling with Intention*, then you don't have to wait! We have designed a unique, virtual sales coaching and training community — **My Sales Coach Now** — that allows you to have instant access to the **sales support that you need, when you need it**!

If you would like to experience the program **FREE for 30 days,** just go directly to **www.mysalescoachnow.com**. All of the details are there. In addition to the training and support, you will also receive a CD in the mail every month so you can also listen in your car. *Don't wait!* **This is the answer you've been looking for!**

Client Success Story!

"Before SCN, I was fearful and very intimidated by selling. After taking advantage of SCN's amazing introductory price and making my way through the $WI Training, I found out that I AM a salesperson after all! Who knew?!? I followed the Principles of Selling with Intention listed in the SWI training step-by-step and IMMEDIATELY saw results!

*I was able to overcome my initial fear of selling, define my target clients, focus on setting appointments, **and land a meeting and first order with my #1 Target Client!** SCN has shown me that selling is easy! It's just a matter of scheduling the time and asking the right questions. Thank you so much! Your services have proven to be invaluable to my development in sales. Thank you, Sales Coach Now!!"*

*Mary Sanchez, Think Ink, **www.thinkinkinfo.com***

If you desire more intensive training or support, then we recommend that you visit **www.salescoachnow.com** to learn more about our *Sales Coach Now Training and Coaching programs.*

While you are on the *Sales Coach Now* home page **(www.salescoachnow.com)**, please sign up for our **FREE Monthly E-Zine** and updates, *"Where Mindset Meets Intention."*

As our **special gift to you**, you will also receive an MP3 Download, *"7 Ways to Sell More in a Doom and Gloom Economy"* just for signing up!